THE BOOK OF
THE DOMESTIC RABBIT

OTHER BOOKS DEALING WITH LIVE HOBBIES
BY THE SAME AUTHOR

Building an Aviary
Soft-Billed Birds
The Book of the Pigeon and of Wild Foreign Doves
The Book of the Racing Pigeon
Making Squab-Raising Profitable

THE BOOK OF
THE DOMESTIC RABBIT

Facts and Theories from Many Sources,
Including the Author's Own Experience

by CARL A. NAETHER

Illustrated

DAVID McKAY COMPANY, INC.
New York

THE BOOK OF THE DOMESTIC RABBIT

COPYRIGHT © 1967 BY CARL A. NAETHER

Third Printing, May 1974

ISBN: 0-679-50138-X

LIBRARY OF CONGRESS CATALOG CARD NUMBER: 67-20182

MANUFACTURED IN THE UNITED STATES OF AMERICA

VAN REES PRESS · NEW YORK

Acknowledgments

The author takes this opportunity to acknowledge the cordial cooperation of all those persons who have helped to make this book possible. In particular he wishes to thank the following for the use of photographs for illustrations: *Deutsche Kleintier Züchter*; Hans Wiedmer; Los Angeles County Fair Association; Helmut Scheide; C. Misset Verlag; J. Messner; Art Ammon; James W. Albaugh; The Harmons and Ernie Gibbs; Adr. de Cock.

Contents

Introduction

*T*he Book of the Domestic Rabbit is meant mainly for hobbyists, both young and not so young, who derive considerable pleasure from keeping and caring for rabbits, whether fancy or utility. These confirmed animal lovers occupy themselves during their leisure hours with building their own hutches and other essential equipment, and, of course, with attending personally and enthusiastically to the various tasks, light and pleasant as they are, conducive to maintaining their rabbits in sound health and breeding condition the year round. And while these hobbyists welcome the occasional sale or exchange of surplus stock, profit-making is not their prime motive in raising rabbits. It is keen enjoyment provided by more or less close, daily handling of their animals —personal satisfaction derived from seeing them grow rapidly and mature normally into fancy or utility stock of high quality.

Having then been written primarily for hobbyists, this book sets forth in simple, informal language the essentials of making a satisfactory start with domestic rabbits, of keeping them in good health by means of proper care and feeding, and of breeding them so as to achieve their owner's set goals and standards, whatever these may be. Technical and scientific matters of breeding, feeding, etc., have been purposely not treated since they presume a thorough familiarity with modern principles of biology, which the average rabbit raiser does not have, and is, moreover, usually reluctant to acquire. Usually he is content to proceed on the basis of his own experience, and on whatever helpful information and advice he may obtain from fellow breeders and from reading magazines and books.

The writing of this book, and particularly the gathering of photographs for its illustrations, have afforded the author a welcome opportunity to relive, so to say, carefree hours of his youth when rabbits were his "passion" before and after school, and also in later life when in partnership with a good friend he kept a sizable herd.

Special thanks are due the editors of the *Deutsche Kleintier Züchter* for providing numerous excellent photographs for illustrations, also to Joachim Schuette and Werner Moebes for their cordial cooperation in furnishing relevant information.

CARL A. NAETHER

Encino, California
January 1967

THE BOOK OF
THE DOMESTIC RABBIT

CHAPTER ONE

Domestic Rabbit Culture, Past and Present

*Origin; domestication; folklore;
relation to hare; hobby or utility;
past and present popularity; use of
meat, fur, and by-products.*

THE domestic rabbit, of which there are now more than sixty-five varieties, is descended from the wild European rabbit, whose scientific name is *Oryctolagus cuniculus*, the term *cuniculus* signifying also underground passage. The word "rabbit" was first applied, about the 15th century, to the young only, and is seemingly derived from the French *rabet*, the Old French being *connin*. The Latin *cuniculus* in various interesting forms may be seen not only in *connin*, but also in the Old English *conyng* and *coney*, the German *Kaninchen*, the Spanish *conejo*, and the Italian *coniglio*.

America is not the native land of the rabbit, which is assumed to have spread from Africa to Spain, Corsica, Sardinia, and Sicily. Spain is regarded as its original home, where its abundance is suggested by its appearance on the Roman-Spanish coins of Emperor Hadrian (117–138 A.D.). In 230 A.D., rabbits found their way into Italy, where soon after being well established, they became quite a delicacy; on fast days it was customary to eat the embryos. The Chinese at the time of Confucius used rabbits in their religious ceremonies.

1

The rabbit, so the report goes, had been domesticated by the first century B.C. According to the Roman scholar Varro, it was kept in so-called *leporaria* or escape-proof, walled-in enclosures. First mention of the modern European rabbit was made by the Greek historian Polybius. Writing about Corsica in the second century B.C., he stated that while there were no hares in Corsica, there were burrowing animals looking like small hares. He called them *kunikloi.* In the 18th century the rabbit hunt was quite fashionable in certain French circles. Casanova in his memoirs deplores the fact that a young woman failed to keep a rendezvous with him, preferring instead to go rabbit hunting with a nobleman!

In folklore and in history, the rabbit has played a prominent part. The stories of Easter bunnies are said to date back to a Teutonic legend, in which the rabbit was once a bird, but was changed to its present form by the goddess Ostara. In appreciation for this unusual service, the rabbit laid eggs for the spring festival of the goddess. Among little-known superstitions is the one that the left hind foot of a rabbit taken into a churchyard at midnight when the moon is full, will shield its owner from evil. A well-known folk tale tells of the race between the hare and the tortoise. At the time of Confucius, the Chinese used rabbits in various religious ceremonies. American Indians have hunted rabbits since early times, utilizing them for food and for clothing. To catch them, they formed circular or V-shaped lines over a wide terrain which abounded in rabbits. Gradually coming toward one another, the hunters herded the rabbits into small space, where they killed them with clubs. In *American Cookery in Household Ord.,* published in 1790, this meaningful sentence occurs: "Then take conynges parboyled or elles rabits, for thai are better for a lorde."

Rabbits, it is well to remember, are distinct from hares, with which they are often confused. Hares are usually larger than rabbits, averaging almost twice their weight. Moreover, their ears, which are black-tipped, are longer, as are also their hind legs. Hares do not as a rule have their young in underground burrows, as do true rabbits. When born, young hares can open their eyes, and they have a full coat of hair, while young rabbits are born blind and naked, and with their ears closed. Their eyes open on the 11th day, and their ears on the 12th day. They are self-supporting when four weeks old. Our North American jackrabbit is really a hare. Contrary to often-voiced rumors, hares and rabbits will not cross.

The keeping of domestic rabbits may serve as a hobby or as a business. Many young people enjoy caring for some rabbits in their backyards. Frequently they are junior members of well-established rabbit or 4-H clubs that further special youth programs. Their hobby of keeping rabbits is thus not likely to become a hit-or-miss affair, but is in fact a well-regulated activity designed to enhance their love and knowledge of animal life through teaching them in thoroughly practical and humane ways the fundamentals of producing better-quality rabbits. Usually the senior members, both at club meetings and at their own rabbitries, are well prepared to provide the incentives as well as the practical advice designed to enable the junior members to make a successful and really enjoyable start with rabbits. The latter will thus be encouraged to keep these gentle animals sufficiently long to learn at first-hand, under direct and more or less expert supervision, the essentials of keeping rabbits in good health and production. Since monetary returns, while desirable, are not the prime purpose of these youngsters' hobby, they are likely to derive daily much keen pleasure and personal satisfaction from discovering and then following the fascinating life cycles of their rabbits through the care and feeding they give them every day. Moreover, being in close touch with fellow junior members, there will be much friendly rivalry,

which is quite likely to strengthen their interest and to enhance their enthusiasm for raising each year better animals,
and perhaps also better ones than their friends are raising.

Only a modest investment is required to obtain some young
rabbits or else a bred doe to serve as a boy's livestock project.
The fast-growing youngsters will give him ample opportunity
to familiarize himself with their feeding and other habits
until they are ready for breeding. If the boy starts with a
bred doe, his interest in the project will greatly increase when
she kindles and begins to raise her lively family. Since he is
not the only club member to keep rabbits, but has friendly
rivals in this fascinating activity, he can strive to surpass
their efforts and ultimately compete for prizes at county fairs
and club shows. An interesting case in point is given in T. A.
Erickson's book, *My Sixty Years with Rural Youth*, in which
the author comments on the 4-H activities of his four chil-
dren, who belonged to the St. Anthony Flyers 4-H Club of
Ramsey County, Minnesota, but particularly on those of his
son Cyrus:

"One of Cy's early projects was raising rabbits, which
accounted for a jar of rabbit meat that he put up as a 4-H
Club member. He bought his first rabbits with his own
money, built hutches for them in the backyard, and once
when they were stolen, he gamely earned the money to start
over with a new pair.

"One day, Cy and Ockie Husby, another eleven-year-old
member of the same 4-H Club, disappeared for so long that
we became worried, for they had forgotten to tell us where
they were going. Cy came in tired and red-faced.

" 'Where have you been?' I said.

" 'Canning,' he said, 'and we beat!'

"They had been in the canning demonstration contest on
Ramsey County's 4-H Achievement Day, and even though

girls of high-school age had also competed, the boys were picked to go to the State Fair."

That girls also are active in the rabbit hobby is indicated by James W. Albaughs, an Ohio fancier, who writes on Kenneth Mauney's page, "The Backyard Rabbitry," in *The National Rabbit Raiser* magazine, in part as follows:

"We have had rabbits for the past six or eight years. Now we have fourteen does and three bucks, plus some young stock, representing registered Red Satins, White Satins, Californians, and New Zealand Reds. The 'we' includes Nancy Rosetta, my twelve-year-old daughter, who is my business partner and a seventh grader at Welty Junior High in New Philadelphia. She takes quite an interest in the rabbits and does a good deal of the feeding and keeping the pens clean.

"I am enclosing two pictures, one of them taken at the Tuscarawas County Fair. Nancy is standing in front of one of our hutches with her Red Satin in front of her on the feed barrel. The other picture shows my niece Marilyn, who won first in her division and showed the reserve grand champion of the Fair, and my daughter Nancy. Nancy won a close second place with her Red Satin. They were two mighty proud girls, I will say.

"Marilyn and her brother David, Jr., age thirteen, have eight does of good stock and are doing quite well with their project. David Junior has shown rabbits at the Fair for the past two years and has received blue ribbons both times.

"We feed pellets once a day, and twice a day to does with litters. For the evening feed our rabbits get a good grade of clover hay. We feed also sweet corn that gets too hard for table use, apples, pears, carrots, beets, turnips, cucumbers, some cabbage, lettuce, spinach, and other vegetables. Of course, this feed must be fresh and fed in small quantities until the rabbits are used to it. We feed also dry bread, which we get in large quantities from a local bakery, and which is a real treat for our rabbits. After using these various kinds of feed for some time, I don't think that we ever lost a rabbit. Our rabbits certainly like variety. In closing, I will say that we get lots of pleasure and enjoyment from our rabbits, and we feel that keeping them is a very worth-while hobby."

Undoubtedly, the most valuable aspect of the juniors' hobby or project, as it is often called, is that it not only teaches them respect for animals, but also gives them a sense of responsibility—the various chores of feeding, breeding, cleaning, and many others must be done regularly and well. I well remember my own rabbit-keeping, which I enjoyed all through my high-school years—remember its daily, satisfying aspects with keen pleasure. My father had given me permission to keep rabbits in our large backyard and garden on *one* condition—that I be wholly responsible for their keep and their well-being. It was clearly understood that no other member of the family would help me with the feeding and numerous other chores required to keep them healthy and productive. Whatever young they raised successfully belonged to me to do with as I liked. In summer, green food was always available in copious quantities, and in winter there were, besides clean hay, carrots, beets, and potatoes in abundance. Occasionally my mother would serve rabbit for the noonday meal, paying me well for this welcome change in the daily family menu.

Many adults keep rabbits as a hobby. Usually they like animals. Daily contact with their rabbits provides outdoor relaxation and a welcome change from work, with release from tensions. Moreover, rabbits are exceedingly prolific (according to Pennant, British zoologist, a single pair of wild rabbits can produce as many as 12,748 in four years!), easy to raise, and require but small space. And what is very important to most rabbit enthusiasts, there is a market for rabbit meat and skins the year round, as well as for live rabbits for laboratory and other uses.

A case in point of how some adults start rabbit raising is furnished by the following account, which was written by Mrs. Ballweg of Pine Bush, New York, for *The National Rabbit Raiser* magazine, and which is here presented in condensed form:

"My husband and I started our rabbitry with one Easter bunny, a doe. Our neighbor also had an Easter bunny, which happened to be a buck; so we were soon in business. My husband made all the hutches, which now are all of uniform size. All our hutches have wire floors, which we believe to be the best for sanitation and also for ventilation, especially on hot days.

"We now have thirty-four working does and an expanding market. We keep only New Zealand Whites, which we supply to laboratories. Our rabbits have water in front of them at all times, and on 90-degree days they are watered two or three times a day. We feed a medicated pellet and thus far have not been troubled with any really serious rabbit disease. To keep our litters warm in winter, we give our does wood shavings for nesting material. It has a clean, fresh smell, and they enjoy digging into it.

"We love working with our rabbits, and there is always something to learn about them. My husband and I work together; he waters them and I feed them. Sometimes we find that a doe cannot take proper care of her litter; so we transfer the babies to another doe. Before doing so, we rub a small bit of Vicks on the doe's nose, and also on the bunnies to be transferred. By the time the smell of Vicks wears off, the litter has taken on the smell of the new mother and she has accepted her foster babies."

Among the qualities which contribute appreciably to the

rabbit's popularity as a meat- and fur-producing animal, or as a pet, is, first of all, its pronounced gentleness. Accorded humane treatment by their keeper, rabbits are not likely to bite. Handled with patience and consideration, they very soon become delightfully tame and let themselves be picked up and fondled by their keeper. Rabbits are silent creatures, so much so in fact as to prompt some people to think they are voiceless, which, however, is not the case. Finally, the domestic rabbit is clean in its habits: unless forced to do so, it will not eat dirty, moldy, greasy, or spoiled food. Only natural, unadulterated foods, rich in vitamins, such as fresh, luscious greens of many kinds; juicy root crops, including beets and carrots; top-quality hays, and various nutritious grains—all these edibles are to its liking. Little wonder that the pearly-white, fine-grained meat of this attractive little animal ranks among the most nutritious and palatable meats available for human consumption.

Today, commercial rabbit raising is widespread in many countries. In some of them it gained impetus during wartime when most kinds of meat became scarce and when food rationing was in effect. In the United States during World Wars I and II, rabbit meat, being delicately flavored, high in protein, and low in fat, was a featured item on daily menus in homes and restaurants. Today, more than sixty-five million pounds of domestic rabbit meat are produced in this country each year. Producers range from small backyard rabbitries, in which fifty or more producing does are kept to yield both leisure-time employment and extra family income, to large-scale, commercial rabbit farms, conveniently equipped and efficiently operated to maintain five hundred or more producing does. These commercial ventures, operated strictly along businesslike lines solely for profit, usually employ a full complement of trained help.

In Europe, particularly in France, where the culinary art

has been notably perfected, rabbit meat has proved popular since 1850, when over seventy million rabbits were produced each year, three million of which found their way regularly to consumers in Paris. In 1875, according to Lord Malmsbury, the industrial center of Nottingham, whose inhabitants were mainly workmen, consumed over three thousand rabbits weekly. At that time, 1.5 million rabbits were shipped weekly from Ostend, Belgium, to England. Since then, rabbit-keeping in England has grown fast, there being over twelve million meat rabbits produced by four thousand rabbit farmers. In some countries rabbit meat is an important export article: Denmark ships approximately six thousand tons of this commodity annually to West Germany.

Next to the meat, the thin skin and the dense, soft fur of the rabbit are suited to many uses. Rabbit fur, commercially known as "coney," has by virtue of immensely improved dressing and dyeing methods been developed into low-priced fur known for its many uses. Since it can be dyed, it is used in large quantities under different trade names to imitate the fur of squirrel, seal, beaver, nutria, chinchilla, muskrat, ermine, and leopard. The Angora Rabbit's very long fur has high commercial value, the white color being most in demand. Owing to its well-known felting properties, rabbit fur constitutes the major proportion of fur used in the manufacture of felt hats. From forty to fifty rabbit skins provide material sufficient for a dozen hats. Rabbit fur finds use also in the manufacture of upholstery.

Rabbit fertilizer serves as a valuable by-product. If the rabbits are fed a properly balanced ration, the nitrogen content of the manure may run well over 2 percent, which exceeds that of most other domestic-animal manures. Rabbit manure is easily mixed with the soil. To retain as much of its fertilizing value as possible, it may be composted for future use. Dried, it may be ground up and then sacked for convenient use and for sale in small lots.

Finally, the use of live rabbits for scientific experimental use should be mentioned. Private and public laboratories, hospitals, colleges, and universities utilize rabbits for research relating to various diseases, nutrition, the effects of drugs, and numerous other health problems.

CHAPTER TWO

Starting with Domestic Rabbits

Methods of buying foundation stock
Characteristics of healthy rabbits
Selecting the right breed
Breed qualities and breed standards

WHEN you buy rabbits to serve as your foundation stock, whether their keeping is to serve as an enjoyable spare-time hobby or as a profitable utility, you should be guided by certain commonsense fundamentals whose observance is most likely to ensure the success of your new venture. To forestall early disappointments and failures occasioned by the loss of ailing animals, poorly producing does, diseases brought on by overcrowding or lack of cleanliness, consider the following suggestions based on practical experience.

First, and perhaps most important of all, try to locate a responsible breeder of the variety you plan keeping, preferably one living in or near your own community. If you are not acquainted with local rabbit farmers, get in touch with your county superintendent of livestock shows, which often include rabbit exhibits. Your county agent or farm adviser may also serve as a source of dependable information. Either one may be able to direct you to local breeders' clubs, some of which function in every state of the Union. Or else write to the secretary of the American Rabbit Breeders' Association, Inc., who maintains headquarters at 4323 Murray Avenue, Pittsburgh, Pa., 15217, and who can furnish you a list of National Specialty Associations operating in different states, each one sponsoring a distinct breed of rabbits. You might consult also the advertising pages of various rabbit and small-stock magazines, usually available at public libraries, for names and addresses of breeders located not too far from your home.

You will gain much by calling in person at a fancier's rabbitry, since there you will have an excellent opportunity to see not only what kind and quality of stock he keeps, but also where he keeps it and how well he cares for it. These, your first impressions of a seller's rabbit culture, which will point also to his personal character, will determine whether or not you decide to buy your foundation stock from him.

In judging the value of rabbits, or for that matter of any kind of livestock, to serve as foundation material, you look above everything else for animals that are in vigorous health. Healthy rabbits are active: at feeding time, especially, they will come to the fronts of their hutches demanding attention. They do not sit more or less listlessly in a corner of the hutch. Their eyes are bright and full; their noses slightly moist, and their ears erect and free from mange. Their forepaws are dry, not soiled with mucus; their feet and tails are straight and well-shaped. Their fur is smooth and sleek. Their weight falls within the limits set by the breed's standard: underweight or potbellied specimens are to be strictly avoided. A rabbit's droppings should be hard, round, and firm. The fur around the anus should be clean, not soiled by droppings.

If, perchance, you plan to go into rabbit raising as a *business*, even on a small scale, then be sure to visit a number of rabbit farms before you buy your foundation stock. Such visits will afford you a very good opportunity to compare the various enterprises and to judge more satisfactorily which of the particular breeds or strains you have seen is likely to meet your own requirements. Do not pay too much attention to breeders' praises of their herds. Rather ask to see some proof in black and white of both profitable production and reproduction. You want foundation material able to produce early-maturing, marketable rabbits of a certain size and top quality at the lowest possible cost. Before you pay out good money—first-class stock is certainly not cheap—ask to see the production records of the animals you have under consideration, including those of the bucks as well as those of the does. If the rabbit farmer tells you that he does not keep such records, or if he is unwilling to show you whatever records he does keep, then you had best not buy any stock from him, since you would not know what you might be getting. A man operating a rabbitry as an established business, large or small, can ill afford not to keep careful records of production and reproduction, that is, *continuous* books by means of various hutch cards, production accounts and summaries, pedigrees, etc. He should certainly have the production record of each breeding animal in his herd in black and white. Only by such businesslike follow-up can he at any given time evaluate the over-all condition of his business, then make from time to time the necessary changes to ensure more and more profitable production at lower costs. The time and the expense devoted to keeping the right sort of records are without question a sound business investment.

In case you have not kept rabbits before, be sure to start on a small scale. Weaned youngsters will enable you to make a worthwhile beginning, since during their growing and maturing periods you can familiarize yourself thoroughly with eating and other habits long before they reach breeding and production age. This experience will give you confidence in handling them and their offspring satisfactorily. You can make a good beginning likewise with one buck and two or three does, keeping their best youngsters for expansion. Most beginners with rabbits make the all-too-common mistake of starting with too many, and of later on having far too many for the available space. Crowding, which certainly increases the necessity for frequent cleaning of hutches, is not at all conducive to the rabbits' health, since it tends to increase the danger of disease. No more rabbits should be kept at any time than can be housed comfortably and cleanly.

When making a start, you will have a choice of numerous different breeds or varieties. Be sure to select one that suits your main purpose best. Keep in mind that there is no all-purpose breed, no single one that is *the* best. If you want rabbits mainly for exhibition purposes or for selling as breeders, then select a popular breed, one for which there is likely to be a good and steady demand in your own community and its adjoining territory. There is a wide variation in the weights and colors of the different breeds. Usually most desirable are early-maturing breeds that produce young with a marketable carcass at eight weeks. The does should be able to raise large litters successfully. Mature animals of the smaller breeds weigh from three to six pounds each, while those of the larger breeds, such as the Flemish Giant, New Zealand, American Chinchilla, and others, weigh from ten to fifteen pounds. Since their skins are usually in steady demand, *white* rabbits, which are good meat producers, are desirable for the beginner. When it comes to wool production, there are the English and the French Angoras, whose individual weight ranges from six to eight pounds. Generally speaking, in the United States, breeds such as the New Zealand Reds and Whites, the American Whites and Blues, the Californians, and the Flemish are extensively kept for meat and fur.

For many beginners the medium-heavy breeds, which include the American Standard Chinchilla, Beveren, Californian, Silver Marten, and others, are very suitable. They mature approximately a month earlier than the heavy breeds, and they require less feed. Until the beginner has accumulated considerable experience, it will be to his advantage to concentrate on only one breed, preferably one with a solid color. He should select bucks and does of the same shade of color, and they should reproduce true to color as well as to type. By purchasing his entire foundation stock from *one* rabbitry, he can make reasonably sure of starting out with rabbits of more or less uniform type and dominant characteristics. Raising a solid-colored breed to meet the requirements of the standard is usually much easier than raising a breed with exacting markings. He should not forget, however, that all breeds have utility, and that with every breed the production of quality meat is usually its greatest utility. For all-round purposes, that breed is best which produces the most and the best-quality meat at the lowest cost of feed. Moreover, to derive a satisfactory profit from the average rabbit enterprise, the returns from both meat and pelts have to be combined.

In the United States, by far the largest number of rabbit raisers are neither 100-percent fanciers nor 100-percent commercial producers, but a combination of both. As a matter of fact, the average fancier is compelled to convert many animals, which for one reason or another fail to meet breed standards or are unfit for breeding, into meat. Moreover, he sells, or else exchanges, many animals for breeding purposes. On the other hand, the commercial breeder finds it to his advantage to patronize rabbit shows and to keep in touch with fanciers with a view to locating animals with which to improve his own strain or strains.

Any beginner intending to breed rabbits principally for show purposes and for sale as breeding stock should by all means obtain the official standard of the desired breed or breeds. He can get this important information from the secretary of the specialty club or association, or else in book form from the American Rabbit Breeders' Association.

The standard enumerates in considerable detail the essential physical requirements which a rabbit belonging to a certain breed should have in order to function as a more or less *typical* representative of that breed. This detailed list of breed characteristics, compiled usually by the committee on standards of a specialty club, functions as the yardstick by which the breed is judged at all shows. It reflects the majority opinion of the membership as to the special physical traits which their breed should in large measure have. Since this judgment is subject to change, so is the standard; hence the beginner should always consult the most recent standard.

He should familiarize himself thoroughly with the provisions of this standard so as to be able to recognize a *typical* New Zealand Red, Californian, etc., when he inspects a certain herd. He should, moreover, pay particular attention to the sections in the standard labeled "Major Faults" and "Minor Faults" in order to avoid buying animals showing serious defects. Most breed standards will emphasize so-called *type*, which is the sum total of those qualities establishing a given productive strain. As the saying goes, "A certain breed produces true to type." The standards will emphasize also *quality*, which reveals the grade of the rabbit and its offspring. Texture of fur, firmness of bone structure, and the all-round finish of the animal stand for quality. *Condition* is another key term found in standards. It relates to the extent to which a rabbit's entire body is covered with flesh. *Conformation* concerns the head, neck, forequarters, body, and hindquarters as structural units of an efficient whole. A faulty unit is likely to weaken the whole body structure. When a judge passes on a rabbit's conformation, he looks for good points as well as for major and minor faults, especially as they may affect its production capacity. Last, but by no means least, comes *Physical Make-Up as a Whole.* A rabbit should be deep, wide, and well coupled in the chest, fore-flank, and loin, with pinching neither behind the shoulders nor in the loin. If it possesses these physical traits in generous measure, it is considered sound and strong.

In evaluating the strain or strains of a breeder's herd, the beginner should not be misled by its boasting a few animals that have won top prizes at shows. Such isolated winnings may not be at all typical of the herd as a whole. He should rather look for a herd of fancy rabbits of *uniform* quality, since this suggests *selective,* carefully planned breeding of really good animals over an extended period of time; then, if possible, purchase from its owner specimens of as excellent type and quality as the latter is willing to sell. Needless to add, most fanciers will not sell their best breeders, or even the offspring of these. The beginner should not rush to the conclusion that by acquiring rabbits which have won honors in the show-room, their young will necessarily show the same, or even similar, high quality. As a beginner in the fancy, he will do well to trust the judgment of a reliable, long-experienced breeder in his community, who is well known for the uniform quality of his herd, as evidenced in part by the reputation he enjoys in the rabbit fancy. Such a man may make show and production records, kept over a period of years, available to a serious prospective purchaser for inspection.

How a successful start was made with rabbits is related in the following account from John and Oreen Hoblitzell, who operate the Hobby's Rabbitry in Tampa, Florida. It appeared in *The National Rabbit Raiser* magazine and is here given in abbreviated form.

"Afraid that the noisy chickens we kept would bring complaints from our neighbors, we decided to raise rabbits, which I (John Hoblitzell) had kept as a youngster. So I went to a rabbit show in Tampa, talked to several breeders, joined the American Rabbit Breeders' Association, and bought two rabbits. That was the beginning of our herd— two Californian does. I had looked at all the breeds exhibited and then decided to raise Californians, because they looked good and they felt good! We pushed them, showed them, and extolled their good qualities on many occasions. It appears that now Californians are being raised more extensively than any other breed in Florida.

"We have approximately four hundred does in our herd at this time and are expanding rapidly. Our rabbits are housed in all-wire hutches, 2½'x4', hung under open sheds 10' wide and 100' long. We use automatic waterers and outside feeders of my own design and manufacture. We find this arrangement to be ideal for the mild Florida climate.

"The demand for good, ranch-raised rabbit meat in this area is tremendous. Most of the processors pay top prices for Californians, considered top-grade utility rabbits. Local rose growers buy all the rabbit manure we can furnish."

Some interesting sidelights on rabbit-keeping in Alaska are provided by E. S. Albright of Fairbanks, who writes in the ARBA *Bulletin* in part as follows:

"I do not raise rabbits for profit, but as a hobby. And my family relishes fried young rabbit. I cross New Zealand White does with Checkered Giant bucks; their offspring produces a large, meaty fryer in a short time. Also I like the array of colors of these crosses, ranging from snow-white with pink eyes to coal-black with black eyes.

"My outdoor pen arrangement for wintering my rabbits consists of a cyclone fence buried a foot deep into the ground and covered with chicken wire to keep out ravens, eagles, owls, and wildcats. The heavy sides are necessary to prevent loose dogs, which often run here in packs, from tearing through them. The rabbits are kept in these pens, where they burrow from September to May. They are fed alfalfa pellets and drink snow water. The temperature of the frozen ground never gets below 31 above zero, even though we have minus 40- to minus 50-degree weather for days at a time. The rabbits come out each day for a short time to feed and to eat snow.

"From May to September my rabbits are kept in conventional hutches, in which they are bred. Usually each one of my does has three litters a year, averaging eight to twelve young per litter. I have found it very impractical to let a litter be born in a burrow. The young turn out as spooky and as wild as snowshoe hares, and they can be caught only either by trapping or by shooting."

CHAPTER THREE

Modern Breeds of Rabbits

Classification—size, utility, kind of fur, etc.
Description of breeds

THE astounding progress which domestic rabbit culture
has made within a relatively short period of time is
clearly shown by the total number of breeds now being
raised, both in this country and in Europe, which stands at
nearly fifty! A breed, or a race, it is well to remember at
this point, refers to a permanent variety or family of animals,
whose members, paired together, will reproduce the distinctive characteristics of shape, size, color, markings, fur texture, growth, etc., which clearly distinguish one particular
group from every other of its kind.

Especially in rabbit culture, a breed is best not thought
of as an absolute class, one which will transmit its inherited
traits perfectly, since many breeds are simply crosses or bas-
tards. Moreover, year after year a breed of rabbits is subject
to various changes, as induced by climatic conditions, methods of feeding and maintenance, and especially by selection
based on the varying provisions of a standard. The standard
enumerates and describes in some detail the essential traits
or qualities of an ideal specimen of the breed; it allots a
given number of points, out of a total of one hundred, to

each trait or quality. Carefully set up by specialist clubs, breed standards are subject to change and revision from time to time, as agreed upon by the club's membership.

When you have had an opportunity to see 14,225 rabbits belonging to 48 different breeds, on exhibition, as was the case not so long ago in Stuttgart, Germany, where two hundred judges officiated, you begin to wonder at the ways in which new breeds may be "created." There is, first of all, *mutation,* a sudden variation in some inheritable characteristic. The Satin Rabbit, a true American breed, which occurred in a litter of Havanas, resulted from mutation. Its hair fiber shows a brilliant sheen, since the scales of the hair are smoothed and the central hollow cells of the hair fiber are eliminated. Other examples of mutations in rabbits are the Lop-ear, the short hair of the Rex, the long hair of the Angora, as well as the black and the white color of the fur. Desirable mutations have then in their original forms been combined with existing breeds to originate new varieties. *Combination,* in other words, both accidental and planned, has been instrumental in adding many new breeds to the already existing number. The white Angora Rabbit originated from a combination of two very old, well-known mutation types—the white, red-eyed Albino and the so-called Longhair Rabbit. More recent "creations" by means of combination will be named and explained in the descriptions of modern breeds which follow. For the reader's convenience, they are given in alphabetical order.

Available space does not permit of describing every breed in minute detail. That is the special function of the official breed standard, which the reader should consult for the particular breed or breeds which have special interest for him. Descriptions in the following listings are meant mainly for ready general identification.

American Rabbit

A hybrid of unknown ancestry, the American Rabbit, boasting a broad, meaty, arched (so-called mandolin) back, was first exhibited in California in 1917, then only in blue. Later on, after some whites appeared in the litters, the breed's popularity grew appreciably.

Weighing from eight to eleven pounds, the American Rabbit, firmly fleshed over its entire body, with especially fleshy hindquarters, has a well-shaped, somewhat narrow head, with ears carried erect, and prominent eyes, which are pink in Whites and blue in Blues. The tail, carried straight, is of the same solid color as the animal's body.

This breed's undercoat should be clear and closely packed, generously intermixed with coarse guard-hairs. In the White phase, the entire body, including head, ears, legs, and feet, should be a clean, pure white. In the Blue phase, a rich, dark, slatey-blue should cover the entire animal evenly and to a considerable depth.

American Chinchilla

The Chinchilla Rabbit is a favorite with many fanciers. Its valuable fur, which closely resembles that of the genuine *Chinchilla lanigera,* and its early (six months) maturing tendency are the principal reasons for its popularity. This popular breed was originated in France in 1913, presumably by crossing Blue Beverens, Himalayans, and wild rabbits, the gray of the last mentioned figuring prominently in this "creation." This attractive exhibition rabbit was brought to the United States in 1919, where it gave the domestic pelt industry an auspicious start. Since then, the texture, color, and density of its fur, as well as its general exhibition and meat-producing qualities, have all been vastly improved.

The silky, blue-gray chinchilla color results from an interplay of dark blue, light and dark gray, grayish or bluish white, and black. A coarse, wavy ticking runs over the back and down the sides. What is wanted in this breed is a glossy, smooth, dense, fine-textured fur.

Three varieties of this excellent fur and exhibition rabbit are being raised in this country: the American Chinchilla, weighing from nine to twelve pounds; the American Giant Chinchilla, weighing from thirteen to fifteen pounds; and the American Standard Chinchilla, weighing from six and a half to seven pounds. The Giant Chinchilla, with its large, powerful body and massive hindquarters, is kept mainly as a commercial meat producer.

American Sable

First produced in 1924 and recognized as a standard breed in 1931, Sables occurred in litters of Chinchillas. The American Sable is larger than the Siamese Sable (so-called because it resembles the Siamese Cat) and of a more uniform color.

A rabbit of medium length, with broad shoulders and hindquarters, and a full chest, the American Sable's fur should be rich sepia-brown on the back, running as far down as possible on the chest, sides, and flank. To blend these parts of the body, the head, ears, feet, and tail should be a brown of purplish shade.

The American Sable is a crossbreed, hence does not reproduce true to color. Light, medium, and dark-colored young may therefore appear in any litter. To obtain typically sable-colored offspring, it is advisable to mate dark-colored with light-colored animals. At the age of seven months, the color of the fur is definitely set. To preserve it as much as possible,

long exposure to direct sunlight should be avoided. The ideal
weight for bucks is eight pounds, and for does it is nine
pounds.

Since breeding the American Sable true to color is at best
a difficult task, presupposing a thorough knowledge of breeding methods, especially as relating to color, continued and
accurate record-keeping, and, above all, a great deal of patience, this variety is not recommended to the novice, who
would soon become discouraged with the results obtained.

The Siamese Sable is smaller than the American Sable, the
ideal weights for senior bucks and does being from five to
seven pounds. Their coloring is a saddle of rich sepia, shading to a paler tone on the flanks and sides. The blending of
colors should be gradual and soft, without noticeable blotches
or streaks.

Angora Rabbit

Because the Angora Rabbit furnishes high-quality wool,
as well as meat, it ranks highest as a utility and commercial
breed. Its exact origin, like that of so many other breeds,
is shrouded in mystery. Cases of long fur, the result of mutations, have occurred among *wild* rabbits. The name "Angora"
was conveniently applied, as likewise to Angora goats, because of this rabbit's long, silky fur. There is no proof that
this breed originated in Angora, a city in Asia Minor.

Angora Rabbits appeared as early as 1723 in France, where
the breed has since been vastly improved, both in quality and
in quantity of wool production. About 1777 it found its way
into England and Germany. Not until the late 1920's were
Angora Rabbits imported from England into the United
States and Canada.

Angoras fall into two separate types—the English and the
French. Both are bred in white, black, blue, and fawn, with
white being by far the preferred color. The ideal weight of

the English Angora is from six to seven pounds, while that of the French Angora runs to over eight pounds. Both types should have compact, well-rounded bodies, with full and round chests. While the wool of the French Angora is coarser than that of the English Angora, it should have uniform length and as much density as possible in both types.

Provided that high-quality wool-producing stock is kept properly, an average annual yield of twelve ounces of wool may be expected from each adult Angora. Naturally, its price will fluctuate with market supply and demand. Some commercial breeders will keep good wool producers on an average of from six to seven years. Angora wool is harvested, usually every three months, electric shears being used for this purpose. While such clipping has the advantage of convenience and speed, and is still widely practiced in many countries, there is also the method of plucking wool, in vogue throughout France. Plucked wool, it is asserted, has more fluff and life than clipped wool, hence demands a more favorable market price. Plucking rabbits, when done by experienced hands, does not hurt the rabbit, provided, of course, that the wool is ripe, for then it comes away easily. Moreover, plucking produces a heavier growth than clipping.

Belgian Hare

No other domestic rabbit suggests in its general appearance the elegance, vitality, and vigor possessed by the Belgian Hare. Its vibrant, graceful form, entirely different from that of any other domestic variety, points unmistakably to an exhibition or show rabbit of the first rank. As such, the Belgian Hare is kept by fanciers who put beauty of form and color before any other trait.

This exciting breed was originated from the common Belgian Landrabbit. It was called "hare" to suggest the form of the wild hare, with which, of course, it has no relation what-soever. Greatly attracted by the beautiful, deep-red color of the Belgian Landrabbits, fanciers in England, having im-ported a considerable number, promptly and enthusiastically set to work to develop the typical, racy hare type. The Bel-gian Hare was a show or exhibition type as far back as 1880, numerous British Belgian Hare clubs testifying to its growing popularity.

To the United States, this unique breed came about 1888. Since that time it has seen periods of great popularity, when high-quality, show-type Belgian Hares would fetch $300 and more apiece. Today the breed is enjoying a modest popularity among dyed-in-the-wool fanciers.

The Belgian Hare carries its long, arched body, supported by long, slender hind legs well off the ground. Its smooth, long, narrow head is topped by fine, thin ears. The hazel eyes are surrounded by circles of white. The ideal weight for senior bucks and does is eight pounds. Highly important and highly valued is the color of the fur, which should be a rich chestnut-red with considerable brilliant black ticking over the back and the hips.

To win awards in the show-room, these alert animals re-quire patient and thorough training long before they face the judge. Moreover, since they are active animals, their hutches should be roomier than those of other breeds, afford-ing the occupants also ample opportunity for jumping.

Beveren

Essentially a commercial, a meat rabbit, hardy, prolific, and fast maturing, the Beveren, named after the city of Beveren in Belgium, and recognized there as a standard breed since 1922, was first promoted in the United States by the Beveren Club in 1930.

Of medium size, with broad, fleshy back and well-rounded hips, the Beveren is bred in white, blue, black, and brown. Its weights range from nine pounds for senior bucks to ten and a half pounds for senior does. In this country, white Beverens are bred in much larger numbers than any of the other color varieties. Their distinguishing characteristic from other white rabbits is the brilliant, deep-blue eyes.

The original Beveren, concerning whose ancestry little is known, was the blue—the *Bleu de Beveren*. In both Belgium and Holland it was highly prized as a first-class meat rabbit, yielding also an excellent, thick, glossy pelt of light lavender-blue. The black and brown Beverens are rarely seen at shows in this country, the brown having been developed in England.

Californian

An American development, the Californian is the result of crossing a Himalayan doe with a Chinchilla buck. Then a buck of this union was mated to a number of New Zealand White does. George West, the originator, exhibited his new breed for the first time in Southgate, California, in 1928. It was standardized in 1939.

Today, the Californian is a well-established, medium-large, all-purpose utility rabbit, its remarkable meatiness being its featured characteristic. Its body is plump and compact; its hips well-rounded; its flesh very firm. Its fur consists of a dense undercoat, topped by coarser guard-hairs. This white, pink-eyed rabbit retains the Himalayan markings on nose, ears, feet, and tail. When the animal is dressed out, these colored spots are discarded, leaving a pure-white fur having good marketability.

Owing to the uniformity of its young, their rapid growth and early maturing, the Californian has become one of the favorite breeds with fanciers as well as with commercial breeders. These qualities have attracted also European fanciers to the Californian. The ideal weight for senior bucks is nine pounds, for senior does nine and a half pounds.

A fairly definite idea of the productiveness of the Californian rabbit, and also of its feed consumption, is gained from the report of two commercial rabbitries specializing in this breed, given below in round figures:

1.	2.
4.7 litters per doe	4 litters per doe
28 young raised per doe each year	25.2 young raised per doe each year
average weight of young at two months was 4.2 lbs.	4 lbs.
total live weight of young: 120 lbs.	100 lbs.
feed per doe and young: 568 lbs.	523 lbs.
feed quantity for each pound of growth: 5.2 lbs.	5.3 lbs.

Champagne D'Argent

The Champagne Silver Rabbit, *Le Lapin Argente De Champagne,* was mentioned for the first time in 1730 in a French country journal. Named after a part of France, it is one of the oldest breeds of domestic rabbits.

Its exact origin cannot be accurately determined. As early as 1765, Silver Rabbits, small and dark-colored, were commonly raised in the Champagne under the name of *Lapin Riche,* which means "Productive Rabbit." Presumably these dark-furred animals were crossed with various mutations occurring among the half-wild "park rabbits" to produce ultimately the Champagne Silver.

Very popular in France, as well as in Switzerland, Holland, and Germany, because of its hardiness, its food economy, and its rapid growth, the Champagne Silver apparently came to the United States in the early 1900's, where today it ranks as a topnotch meat producer and desirable exhibition animal.

The standard specifies a medium-long body, with well-developed shoulders and hindquarters—a well-balanced, compact, rather fine-boned animal with a high dress-out percentage of firm meat. A good-quality, fast-maturing Champagne Silver, at two months of age weighs from three to four pounds; at four months, six and a half pounds; at eight months, nine and three-quarters pounds; and at ten months, ten and a half pounds.

The young of this excellent utility breed are born black, gradually silvering out over a period of three months. The rich silver sheen, which makes this breed so appealing to many fanciers, consists, first of all, of an intense, dark, slate-blue undercolor, which lends the fur the necessary vitality and solidity. The surface color, approximately ⅜" deep, should be a light ultramarine and as uniform as possible. There should be also a generous sprinkling of long, black guard-hairs over the whole body. The characteristic color pattern of the Champagne Silver can be perpetuated only by pairing members of a long-established strain or family having the correct shade of color.

Among subvarieties may be mentioned the Crême D'Argents, somewhat smaller than the preceding variety. Their surface color is creamy-white with an orange cast, their undercolor a rich orange. The whole coat is to be interspersed with orange guard-hairs. Other subvarieties, more or less popular with English breeders, include the *Argente Bleu,* smaller than the Champagne, its fur having a lavender-blue undercolor, and the *Argente Brun,* which is silver-brown.

Checkered Giant

The Checkered Giant is a heavy meat rabbit, with distinctive color markings. Weights for senior bucks exceed eleven pounds; those for does, twelve pounds. Because of its striking color pattern, this breed is found in numerous American rabbitries today. It was imported from Germany in considerable numbers after 1908, the year in which the German Checkered Giant was declared a standard breed. The Germans, it is interesting to note, obtained their first Checkered Giants from Belgium, where checkered rabbits, often called Belgian Landrabbits, were widely kept during the 16th century.

Our American Checkered Giant has a long, smooth, arched body which is carried off the ground so as to reveal the markings. Its color pattern calls for colored ears, eye-circles with cheek spots below, and a butterfly-shaped nose. Side markings consist of two medium-sized spots, or else two groups of spots on the hindquarters, which should be as nearly alike as possible on both sides. The unbroken spine marking should run from the ear-base to the tip of the tail. The ears should be solidly marked from the tip to the base.

This massive rabbit is bred in black and in blue, the black animals showing much more contrast. The important markings are apparent at birth. So as to keep the colors pure, blacks and blues should be kept separately. Since blues paired to blues produce offspring with faded markings, blues should always be mated with blacks.

Dutch Rabbit

This very attractive breed is, thanks to its fantastic color pattern, one of the most popular ones: at all shows it is well represented, attracting many admirers. It is bred in black, blue, chocolate, tortoise, gray, steel-gray, brown, yellow-gold, and still other colors. Weighing only from three and a half to five and a half pounds, it is the ideal variety for the fancier with limited space. It usually produces large litters, even though it is best not to leave more than six young with a doe. So well do Dutch does nurse their offspring that they are often made to serve as foster mothers for larger breeds. In short, highly-contrasting color markings, small size, and pro-lificness have made the Dutch rabbit a most popular breed, not only in the United States, but in many countries of Europe.

Very probably, the principal ancestor of the Dutch Rabbit was the Brabanco, a medium-large rabbit raised extensively for meat in the former Dutch province of Brabant. The typical Dutch Rabbit pattern existed already in the 16th century. In the 1830's, large numbers of so-called Brabacon Dwarfs, a checkered breed, were imported into England as meat rabbits. There, over many years, they were remarkably improved until finally the Dutch Rabbit, a small animal with a great deal of white and a color pattern still imperfect, emerged.

Today's Dutch Rabbit should have a short, compact body with well-rounded hindquarters and markings forming a symmetrical pattern. The latter should appear clean-cut and as sharply defined as possible. Collar, chest, forelegs, blaze, and foot-stops should be white in all varieties. The fur of this beautiful breed should be lustrous, short, and dense. All other parts should be colored.

This rabbit is bred in many colors today, as enumerated above, with black, showing desirable contrast, being the most popular. A uniform jet-black, very glossy, blending into a slate-blue undercolor is wanted. In blues, a glossy, uniform dark-blue, blending into a slate-blue undercolor, is the correct pattern. In the chocolate phase, a chocolate brown, uniform, glossy, and dark, blends into a bluish undercolor. In the tortoise variety, a bright-orange surface color shades to a smoky blue over the rump and blends with a dark-cream undercolor. Steel-gray specimens are colored steel-gray, interspersed with light-gray guard-hairs, the whole blending into a slate-blue undercolor. The gray Dutch are of a dark shade, with a slate-blue undercolor. There is also a three-colored variety, called Japanese.

Breeding Dutch Rabbits true to the standard is not at all easy, owing to the exacting color patterns. Only specific information of the true ancestry of pairs to be mated is likely to bring reasonably satisfactory results. Fortunately, this breed throws large litters, thus giving the fancier ample opportunity for wide selections. Mismarked young will show up at an early age, usually from three to four days, when they can be removed.

To obtain satisfactory breeding results with Dutch Rabbits, carefully-planned linebreeding and also inbreeding are most likely to prove effective. Animals having similar faults should not be mated. In most cases, it is best to pair Dutch having the same color pattern. However, real improvement in the particular pattern can be expected only by mating a buck or a doe with near-perfect markings to another of the same color pattern with as good markings as possible. First litters are often not very satisfactory, so that it becomes needful the following year to mate the best-marked young back to either or both parents. To avoid getting faded markings, different colors are sometimes paired, such as black with blue, resulting in this case in offspring showing greater color intensity.

The novice is advised to confine his keeping of Dutch Rabbits to a single color pattern, at least until such a time as through experience and study he has gathered sufficient practical information to enable him to avoid major blunders likely to make him dissatisfied with this very handsome, popular breed.

English Spot

The English Spot, one of the oldest exclusively fancy breeds, was for many years very popular in its native country, where it reigned at one time as the most valuable exhibition or show rabbit. It was gradually developed from checkered domestic rabbits, which were common in England. In 1885, the breed was exhibited officially for the first time. In America, the number of English Spot enthusiasts is rather limited. This interesting rabbit is bred in black, blue, chocolate, gray, tortoise, and lilac.

Since its distinctive and rather delicate color pattern is quite difficult to achieve in all its exacting details, the English Spot is most surely the breed for the experienced fancier, who, undismayed by repeated setbacks, continues to welcome the challenge posed by its demanding standard requirements. Only after long years of patient study of the Spot's varying breeding peculiarities, coupled with a patient, intelligent application of proven breeding techniques can the fancier expect to produce some English Spots boasting genuine exhibition quality.

A "racy" body, with well-arched back and deep hips, carried well off the ground, typifies the English Spot. Senior bucks and does of this breed weigh from six to eight pounds. The fur of this fancy rabbit, short and sleek, has a pure-white undercolor. In blacks, it should be as lustrous as possible; in blues, as dark as possible; in chocolates, a glossy, dark brown; in grays, as dark as possible; in the tortoise type, bright orange, turning smoky on loins and ears; and in lilacs, an even, pinky dove color.

The markings of the English Spot are found on the head, spine, and sides. Head markings include the butterfly, eye-circles, cheek spots, and color of the ears. The butterfly, the most essential marking, is the crowning feature of this breed. The wings of the butterfly should be well-rounded and include the lower jaw. Eye-circles should be small, even, and closed. The cheek spots should not be too large, unconnected, and either round or oval. The ear color should be sharply defined at the base and should run to the very top.

Back or spine markings include a "herring-bone" stripe over the back, running in even width and unbroken line to the top of the tail. The side markings include the chain, the body, and the loin markings. The chain begins at the ear-base with one pea-sized spot, then descends toward the stomach; the body markings circle up toward the saddle. At the haunches they are joined by the hip markings. As the spots run toward the back, they should get larger, with the largest, about the size of a dime, appearing in the center of the hip. Both sides of the rabbit should be marked alike. A careful study of the current standard of this unique exhibition breed will disclose the numerous exacting and very detailed requirements set for exhibition animals.

In breeding the English Spot, it is not advisable to mix color patterns. One pronounced advantage which the breeder of this variety has is that the various markings are clearly apparent at birth. In other words, mismarked young need not be raised, thus effecting a substantial saving in the cost of both feed and maintenance.

Flemish Giant

The Flemish Giant, which is bred in steel-gray, light-gray, sandy, black, blue, white, and fawn, ranks first in size among the breeds of domestic rabbits. It weighs up to fifteen pounds, and it furnishes the largest pelt. At shows this true giant attracts much favorable attention.

The exact origin of this breed is not known. Apparently this giant was evolved from a mutation occurring among so-called landrabbits, which were extensively raised in Flanders, Belgium, where in 1800 the number of these jumbo rabbits rose to over 15,000! Writing in 1889, K. W. Knight, English rabbit authority, names the Patagonian, "a noble-looking animal" weighing, from twelve to sixteen pounds, and also the Belgian Hare, both imported into England from France and Belgium, as having figured prominently in the early development of the Flemish Giant.

Attracted by the magnificent size, German fanciers saw promising possibilities in a further development of the breed, high-quality specimens of which they imported in large numbers. Laying special and continued stress on size and weight, rather than on fur and color, they finally produced a type which exceeded the old Flemish Giant, both in length and in weight. In 1957 they named this improved product the German Giant. Since that time many of these heavy rabbits have found their way into American rabbitries, where to this day they are kept and raised under the original name of Flemish Giant.

So far as appearance and type are concerned, the Flemish Giant is a broad-chested, long-bodied animal, with correspondingly long, heavy-boned limbs and massive hindquarters, solidly covered with firm flesh. Its head, ears, and limbs should be of a size to harmonize with the length of its body in order to effect a well-balanced, typy whole. Does should have a large, evenly-carried dewlap.

Hutch accommodations for these giant rabbits should measure 3' x 4' for bucks, and 4' x 6' for does, and be from 18" to 24" high. To avoid injuries caused by fighting, Flemish Giant fanciers separate the young after weaning.

Of the various colors in which this variety is bred, gray

has always been one of the most popular, steel-gray in particular. The thick, soft fur should be interspersed with sound, dark ticking, which greatly enhances the rabbit's appearance. Usually satisfactory grays are obtained by mating a high-quality, dark-gray buck to a doe of lighter gray. For specific color requirements, the reader should refer to the current Standard of Perfection.

Harlequin or Japanese

If you like to try your hand at color-breeding and if you can muster the needed knowledge, experience, and patience, you might well consider the Harlequin, the rabbit with the most spectacular color pattern. So unpredictable are the markings in the litters of this fantastic breed that among a hundred young, rarely are two marked alike! In other words, every single litter brings surprises—oddly marked, colorful Harlequins wholly unexpected.

As is true of so many other domestic breeds, the origin of the Harlequin, called Japanese Rabbit by European fanciers for no known reason, is very much beclouded. Rumor has it that this very old French breed, which was exhibited for the first time in 1887 in Paris, descended from a cross of Dutch-marked rabbits with various mutations of the common domestic rabbit. To this day, the Harlequin, or Japanese, Rabbit is raised extensively in Holland, Germany, England, and France. By greatly improving color and markings, the Germans succeeded in producing the beautiful black-and-yellow variety as we have it today.

The Harlequin should have a cylindrical body of even width, front and rear. The breast should be moderately wide and the back moderately long. Mature specimens should weigh about eight pounds. The medium-long fur should have a dense undercoat and fine, even ticking. Black and yellow, or black and gold, as preferred by American breeders, should not merge or mix, but be distinctly separate so as to provide the much-desired contrast. The black-and-yellow, fairly large stripes should appear regularly over the entire body. The more stripes there are, the better quality the specimen. At least four color stripes should appear on each side of the body. The black should be an intense jet-black; the yellow may run to orange, even to fox-red.

Young Harlequins reach their normal weight at between five and six months of age, at which time they are ready for fattening. Does are usually bred at seven months and bucks at nine months. Youngsters with the sharpest defined color pattern are selected from the litters to serve as future exhibition animals or as breeders, or both. Usually the patterns are recognizable a few days after the young are born. They are kept with their mothers eight to ten weeks.

The fancier's aim is to produce a parti-colored head with clearly defined, alternating black-and-yellow or black-and-gold stripes for especially strong contrast. It should be black on one side and orange or yellow on the other. One ear should be black, the other orange or yellow. One front leg should be black, the other orange or yellow. The color of the hind legs should be the reverse of that of the front legs. Among the color patterns bred currently are black and golden orange (or white); blue and golden fawn (or white); brown and golden orange (or white); lilac and golden fawn (or white).

Havana

The Havana Rabbit, prized for its rather rare brown fur, hails from Holland, where its first public exhibition occurred in 1899, in the city of Utrecht. By the early 1900's it was raised in many European countries in large numbers, which, however, decreased rapidly when the rather formidable difficulties of achieving the right color pattern appeared. To the United States, this lovely brown rabbit did not come until 1916. The two types, the standard and the heavyweight, are alike in all respects except their weight, the ideal for the standard Havana being six pounds and for the heavyweight Havana, which is less popular, nine pounds.

A blocky, compact body, with a short, full head, a broad, well-rounded breast, and a wide, straight back, characterizes the Havana's type. However, it is the dense brown fur which sets this breed apart from every other. While the Havana's brown may range from light to dark, almost black-brown, it is the rich, medium-dark brown which is the most desirable and valuable. As a surface color, this shade of brown should run over the entire body. Of great importance is the undercolor—a solid, deep-blue reaching to the skin. These two colors should appear separate from each other. Since the color pattern of the Havana is apparent at birth, those young being too light can be removed at that time, while those having a dense, dark undercolor, with its darkening effect on the surface color, should be kept.

The difficulties encountered in breeding Havanas at all true to the standard of perfection have greatly lessened the popularity which they temporarily enjoyed at one time, both in this country and abroad. The average fancier is usually reluctant to devote many years to experimenting with carefully selected matings of whose ancestry, especially their color inheritance, he must keep careful record. In other words, the Havana Rabbit is the breed for the specialist, who pairs up only animals having a dense, dark-brown surface color and, what is even more important, a rich, deep-blue undercolor.

Himalayan

The individual, jet-black markings against a snow-white background prompted fanciers to name this trim-bodied, rather slim rabbit Himalayan, Russian, Chinese, and Egyptian. None of these appellations point to the true country of origin. In all probability, this rabbit's development took place in England and France about 1850, as a result of mutations and various crossbreedings. By 1895 the breed was well established in Switzerland.

In the handsome Himalayan we have a rather small, trim rabbit, weighing about three and a quarter pounds, with a round, fairly compact body, even back-line, and well-rounded hindquarters. It carries its longish head close to the body. The eyes are bright pink.

Strictly a fancy breed, the Himalayan's appeal to the breeder lies in its distinctive color pattern—the soft, white fur, set off strongly by a black ear, black nose, black feet, black tail, and ruby-red eyes. While in the United States we breed only the black variety, in Europe blue and brown Himalayans also are kept.

Young Himalayans do not show any markings until about the third week, when the nose begins to darken; in the fourth week, the tail and legs also color up. The color pattern is not complete until the young are five months old. A peculiarity of this breed is its pronounced sensitivity to temperatures. Exposed to heat, the black will fade, while exposure to cold will intensify the black markings. Himalayans should not be kept in direct sunlight, where the white will turn yellowish. According to a German writer, if the white fur on any given part of this rabbit's body is shaved off, then given opportunity to grow back in cold weather, black in place of white hairs will appear!

An important point for breeders of the Himalayan to keep in mind—the more time the young require to attain the adult color pattern, the more intense will the colors be. Hence for really successful color breeding, it is best to use animals that require the longest time for their color change.

Lilac

Lilacs were first exhibited in London, England, in 1913, by geneticist Onslow. In 1922 they appeared among a litter produced by crossing the Blue Beveren with the Havana.

This very compact, blocky, and well-rounded rabbit has a fur of outstanding quality. Approximately one inch long and dense, it is a pleasing dove-gray. More specifically, the top color is a soft light-blue or blue-gray with a Havana tinge. This brown tinge must not be too prominent, else it tends to obscure the blue. The most propitious time to exhibit this beautiful rabbit is when it has reached the age of eight months, for then its fur shows top-quality development.

Lops

A rarity at most shows, where they attract many viewers, Lop-ears—there are English, French, and German varieties—appeared in England in 1810 for the first time as "half-lops." So highly esteemed were these quaint-looking rabbits that they became the only and national exhibition race in England for many years. Kempster W. Knight devoted all of *fifty* pages of text to this breed in his fascinating treatise, *The Book of the Rabbit,* the second edition of which appeared in 1889.

When it was discovered that even warmth contributed to the growth of the ears, heated greenhouses, even horse stables, were used for keeping Lops. However, since this practice tended to reduce the animals' resistance to changes in temperature, it was soon abandoned. While Lops are not kept in artificial heat today, their hutches should be comfortably warm. Summer is the best time in which to breed Lops.

Today's standard sets the ear length at eighteen inches or over, and the width of the ear at the widest point at six and a half inches. The ears should be soft and pliable. Their growth is usually complete between the fifth and the sixth month. Ideal weights are ten pounds for senior bucks and eleven pounds for senior does. The English Lop has a medium-long body, a broad breast, arched back, and well-rounded hindquarters. It is bred in solid (self) and broken colors, affording keepers a wide choice. Lops should have large, commodious hutches with plenty of dry, clean litter to keep them warm. Does are bred at nine months. Good results are usually obtained by leaving not more than five or six young with the nursing doe. To avoid any damage to the ears because of fighting, the young should be kept separately following weaning.

The *French Lop* was developed from the English Lop. Its distinctive features are a bold, massive head, carried high, and shorter ears, from sixteen to twenty inches long. Ideal weights for the senior bucks are ten pounds, and eleven pounds for senior does.

German Lops, developed from the French variety, and considered a utility breed, tip the scales at twelve pounds. Ear length ranges from fifteen to sixteen inches. The young have erect ears until their seventh or eighth week. Favorite colors are various shades of gray.

Another German variety, called the *Meissener Lop* after the town in which its originator lived, is characterized by the silver hairs which intersperse the black, blue, yellow, brown, or Havana colors in which this Lop is bred. The ears measure about fifteen inches, and the weight of this Lop is about ten pounds.

Finally, enterprising rabbit enthusiasts in Germany are busy developing a so-called *Miniature Lop,* a very lively animal, weighing only five pounds. Except for its diminutive size, it is the counterpart of the large German Lop, mentioned above. All its physical features are to be well proportioned to its small body so as to contribute to a distinctly harmonious whole.

New Zealand

A strictly American creation, the New Zealand Rabbit (the name carries no special meaning) typifies in every important aspect of its form and body, as well as in the quality of its fur, the American ideal of a topnotch commercial or meat rabbit. Bred in red, white, and black, it is seen frequently at shows. The standard of perfection is the same for all three colors, except for the color of the fur, eyes, and toenails. Ideal body length for bucks should be 18½ inches, for does 19½ inches. Senior bucks should weigh ten pounds; senior does, eleven pounds.

The Red New Zealand, the oldest of the three color phases, appeared in the early 1900's. It was developed from a cross between the Belgian Hare and the Golden Fawn. The White New Zealand, a very popular commercial and show rabbit, appeared in 1920. Its rapid-growth tendencies—at two months it will weigh from four to four and a half pounds—stamp it a most logical breed for commercial use. The Black New Zealand, started in California in 1949 and standardized in 1958, is the newest color phase.

Every important physical characteristic of the New Zealand Rabbit should point to an outstanding utility animal: a blocky, medium-long body, well-filled-in loins, full hips, a very wide back, and well-developed hindquarters, each part firmly fleshed. The fur should be very dense, neither too short nor too soft, interspersed with heavy guard-hairs, and there should be a thick undercoat.

Rabbit-keepers in many parts of Europe, especially in England, Germany, and Holland, have not been long in recognizing and realizing the acknowledged commercial possibilities of the New Zealand Rabbit, as evidenced by the steadily increasing popularity which it enjoys in these rabbit-loving countries.

Palomino

A fairly recent breed, the result of crossing numerous different hybrids, the Palomino is bred in two color patterns— lynx and golden. This rabbit is of medium length, with well-developed hips, loins, and shoulders. Kept principally for meat-producing purposes, it is finely fleshed over its whole body. Its fur is neither wiry nor fine; its undercoat is soft and dense.

The color pattern of the lynx Palomino is a golden-orange over a white undercoat. The surface of the fur is tipped with lilac. The golden variety's fur is a golden-cream, with a creamy white undercoat. Senior bucks weigh from nine to ten pounds; senior does, from ten to eleven pounds.

Polish

Strictly a toy and a fancy breed, the Polish Rabbit is a sprightly, vivacious little animal whose cheerful temperament endears it to any lover of animals. It is frequently used in vaudeville acts, particularly by magicians, who value both its handsome appearance and its small size.

The origin of this miniature breed, as well as that of its name, is not known. The Polish Rabbit was first exhibited in 1884 in Hull, England, where it drew much enthusiastic comment. The Germans call it "Hermelin," because its pure-white fur resembles that of the ermine.

Weighing only two and a half pounds, the Polish Rabbit is short and compact in body. Its furred ears, held stiffly erect, are very thin. Its short, glossy fur is soft and thick. White Polish are bred with either ruby eyes or blue eyes; they are the popular colors, while chocolate and black are not often seen at exhibitions. Rabbit lovers with limited space at their disposal find the Polish Rabbit well suited to their needs.

Rex

To the Abbé Amédé Gillet, who lived in Coulongé, France, belongs the credit of having developed, about 1919, a strain of domestic rabbits, based on a mutation found among a litter of Belgian Hares, boasting a short, plushlike, soft, and upright fur. He named it Castor Rex: Castor, the name for beaver, because its dark-brown fur resembled that of the beaver, and Rex, the Latin for king, as being the "king" of all breeds of rabbits.

The Rex character consists of a shortening of the guard-hairs until they are below or else level with the undercoat, thus effecting a velvety, plushlike coat of nearly one-half inch length. While the fur of all other common varieties of rabbits has the usual upper coat, the Rex fur has none; hence the name "short-haired rabbit." This short, lustrous fur is very thick, silky, upright, and straight, the ideal length being about ⅝". Another distinctive Rex character is the short, curly whiskers.

When the Rex breed made its debut at shows in various countries, it excited much curiosity owing largely to the financial prospects dormant in the sale of its pelt, then considered at least twice as valuable as any ordinary rabbit pelt. High-grade breeding stock, at best very scarce at that time, brought truly fantastic prices. Fanciers in England, Germany, Holland, France, and other countries set about in earnest to perfect the type and the fur, which task required many years. In the United States, the Rex standard was not recognized until 1931.

Today finds this unique, short-haired breed well established wherever domestic rabbits are kept. The Rex is considered as principally a fur rabbit, even though its substantial carcass yields a considerable quantity of firm, solid meat. It is a medium-long animal, with well-rounded hips, well-filled loins and shoulders. Its back is broad and firm. Since Rex fur is at its best quality when the animal is mature, it must be kept for from six to eight months before pelting. Ideal weights for senior bucks are eight pounds; for senior does, nine pounds.

As indicated by the following list, many of the normal-furred varieties have been used to produce interesting-color Rexes. For a detailed description of each color phase, the reader should consult the latest Standard of Perfection. The colors of Rex varieties suggest the following groups: self Rexes, with uniform or about-uniform color over the entire body; shaded Rexes, with darker saddle, shading to lighter color on the flanks; agouti Rexes, with hairs banded with different colors; and tan-pattern Rexes, with self-colored backs and light-colored bellies.

Rex colors run as follows:

Black—a lustrous jet-black over the whole body.
Blue—a rich, lustrous blue over the whole body.
Castor—dark-chestnut or mahogany-brown. Intermediate color rufus-red, sharply defined, over a slate-blue undercolor. Fur lightly tipped with black.

Chinchilla—deep-gray and sparkling. Intermediate color white, with slate-blue undercolor.

Californian—body pure-white, except for nose, ears, feet, and tail; these to be as dark as possible.

Havana—rich chocolate-brown. Undercolor dove-gray.

Lilac—pinkish dove-gray; with ample sheen.

Lynx—intermediate color bright-orange, clearly defined, over a white undercolor. Fur lightly tipped with lilac.

Red—deep reddish-buff over all, with no shading.

Sable—sepia-brown, shading to chestnut on the flanks. Chest to match flanks. Head, ears, legs, and upper side of tail to match saddle.

Seal—dark, almost black, sepia. Slightly paler on flanks, chest, and belly.

White—pure-white, without any yellow or gray cast, over entire body.

Satin

The beauty of this American breed, which appeared first in 1931 as a mutation in a litter of Havanas, lies wholly in the lustrous, satin-like texture and sheen of its fur. This remarkable sheen is produced by translucent hair-shells which act as reflectors of light. High-quality Satin fur is very dense, with a thick undercoat interspersed with small, coarser, shiny guard-hairs; its length should be uniform, from 1″ to 1⅛″. Satins are bred in the following color patterns: white, Californian, black, blue, copper, chinchilla, red, and Siamese.

By virtue of its rich color pattern, the Satin has become a favorite show variety, for which two separate fur classes have been established: one for white and the other for colored animals. The former includes White Satins and Californians; the latter, the remaining color patterns, as listed above. Each individual color is judged according to the latest Satin standard.

As to type, the Satin Rabbit is a blocky, medium-long animal, with full, well-rounded hips, and a fleshy saddle. Ideal weights are nine pounds for senior bucks, and nine and a half pounds for senior does.

Silver

Silver Rabbits are bred in gray, fawn, and brown. The silvering, characteristic of this breed, a white ticking covering the whole body, consists of a diminution of pigment in the secondary guard-hairs. It appears after the first molt, when the rabbits are from four to six weeks old, and requires as long as six months for its completion, varying with individual specimens.

Silvers were first shown in England in 1860. They gained great popularity in that country, also in France. Knight, in *The Book of the Rabbit,* second edition, published in London in 1889, devotes an unusual amount of space to this then much-sought-after breed. He writes in part, "The Silver-Grays are no doubt the Adam and the Eve of all our Silver varieties. Their colour should be, first, a pale skin colour (very slight); then a very rich *blue-slate* colour. The whole is tipped with white silvering and black ticking; this, with the blue shade showing through, gives to this breed its unique appearance. There are three shades: light, medium, and dark. . . ."

The Silver Rabbit has a short, plump, very compact body, with firm flesh. Its coat has an especially tight fit. Weights range from four to seven pounds. Of the three color patterns named above, the gray is by far the most commonly kept. Actually, it is a black-and-white color combination. The body color is black mixed with silver hairs evenly distributed over head, ears, feet, and tail. By far the most important and the most valuable aspect of the silvering, whether it be light, medium, or dark shade, is *evenness*.

The Silver Fawn is a deep, bright orange over the body, head, ears, feet, and tail. Knight calls this color pattern also Silver-Cream, emphasizing the qualities of its fur as being close, compact, very soft and silky to the touch. "The whole body must be evenly ticked with light-colored fawn (not black) hairs, thus giving that beautiful frosted, sharp appearance."

In the Brown Silvers, the important color is a deep, bright chestnut, the undercolor a slate-blue. The white hairs or silvering should be distributed as evenly as possible among the colored ones. The ticking also should be as uniform all over the rabbit. On the surface, brown, white, and black in like proportions should be in evidence.

In selecting breeding stock, try to obtain the very best you can, particularly as to evenness of silvering, and in general, as to color uniformity from nose to tail. Young Silvers begin to change their color at the age of from five to six weeks, the process lasting several months—and fascinating to watch! At six months, the silvering is usually completed.

Silver Fox

This crossbreed was shown for the first time in 1928, having been admitted to the standard of perfection in 1925. As its name suggests, it was "created" to resemble, as closely as possible, the long fur of the wild fox, which, of course, is practically impossible. So the current standard of the Silver Fox Rabbit contents itself with specifying "fairly long fur," which at best is vague.

At any rate, we have in the Silver Fox a broad-bodied, meaty animal, with slightly arched back, weighing from eight to twelve pounds. It is bred in black, that is, jet-black with a slate-gray undercolor; also in dark-blue with a blue-gray undercolor. Most important from an exhibition standpoint is the surface silvering, which should cover the whole body, including belly, head, ears, feet, and tail, and which may be of light, medium, or heavy shade. Above everything else, the silvering should be distributed as uniformly as possible over the entire body. To achieve this ideal requires a thorough knowledge of the characteristics of this breed, especially as it pertains to color inheritance; much skill in pairing up the right animals; and great patience in waiting for satisfactory results, which quite often are slow in materializing.

Silver Marten

Among the principal requirements set by the standard of the Silver Marten, which is bred in black, blue, chocolate, and sable, and which is a hybrid whose exact origin is vague, are the following:

A compact body, with meaty back and shoulders, whose ideal length, measured from tip of nose to base of tail, is seventeen inches for bucks and eighteen inches for does. The ideal weight is seven and a half-pounds for senior bucks, and eight and a half pounds for senior does.

Of the four color phases, the blacks are bred in the largest numbers. A bright and glossy fur, very thick, with guard-hairs somewhat coarser than the undercoat, is characteristic of the Silver Marten. It should be of the same length over the entire body.

The black variety should be jet-black, the fur interspersed with silver-tipped guard-hairs uniformly distributed over the whole body, sides, and hips. The jet-black undercolor should merge at the base into a rich blue.

The blue variety's fur should show an even shade of blue, interspersed evenly with silver-tipped guard-hairs over the whole body.

The chocolate variety features a medium dark-brown chocolate with silver-tipped guard-hairs evenly spread over the whole body. Surface color and undercolor are the same.

The sable has ears, face, and tail a dark sepia-brown. The saddle is medium sepia-brown. The chest, flanks, rump, and feet are ticked with silver guard-hairs. Across the forehead, just below the ears, runs a one-inch-wide light-sepia band.

All colors have a silver triangle at the nape, not over two and a half inches long, connected by a narrow, silver-white band around the neck to the silver-white lower jaw. When selecting Silver Martens for breeding, those having the most distinctly and the most uniformly distributed silver-tipped guard-hairs over the whole body should be given the preference, provided, of course, they show no mealiness.

Tans

A colorful fancy variety, the Tans were first produced in England in the 1880's, then in only one color—black. Now they are available also in blue, chocolate, and lilac. The fundamental Tan pattern consists of a self-colored back with a light-colored belly and tan flanks. The Tan is said to have originated from the wild agouti as a mutation.

Weighing only from four to six pounds, the Tan has a cobby, compact body. Its fur, very close and very glossy, provides sharp and striking contrast against the reddish-tan markings. For silkiness of texture, for density and luster, few other breeds' fur compares with that of the Tan Rabbit.

For the black variety, the standard prescribes a lustrous

jet-black carried well down the hair-shaft. Of the four colors, the black-and-tan, which was the original Tan, is the most popular. Blue Tans should have a shiny slate-blue, spread evenly over the whole body. Chocolate Tans are marked by a lustrous chocolate-brown, spread uniformly over the whole body, with ears and feet matching the body color. In the lilacs, the overall color is a smooth, shiny dove-gray, each hair-tip tinted pinkish. Nostrils, jowl, chest, belly, flanks, and underside of tail should shine brightly with a golden, somewhat reddish, tan, clearly separate from the body color. Tan should appear also in the neck immediately behind the ears, then taper off to a fine point toward the shoulders, thus forming a sort of triangle. The base of the triangle behind the ears should run down to meet the tan on the chest. The ears should be laced with tan on the inside. While all four colors have much in common, each one has its peculiar charm; each one can therefore furnish ample scope for the skill of the breeder.

Because Tan Rabbits are comparatively small, they can be kept in limited quarters. Being docile, they are easy to handle. Given proper food and care, does nurse their young well. The gradual change which the pale-colored youngsters undergo before assuming the lovely, contrasting color pattern of adults is a fascinating process to observe. It may last up to four months, varying with individual specimens.

Viennese

Primarily a commercial breed, the Viennese Rabbit by virtue of its solid, rectangular shape at once suggests the meat type; its pelt has excellent texture and a deep, dense undercoat, thus adding to the animal's utility. In this much-kept rabbit we have a cobby heavyweight, with wide breast, broad, medium-long back, whose ideal weight for senior bucks at eight months runs from nine to ten pounds, and for senior does to from ten to eleven pounds.

While the exact origin of this popular utility rabbit is not clearly known, it was shown officially for the first time in 1895 in Vienna, where it found many admirers and followers. Soon many English fanciers interested themselves in the improvement of this promising breed. They reduced its weight noticeably, calling these smaller rabbits "Imperials." By that name they were exported to Germany, where they were enthusiastically received, and where in due course of time every intelligent effort was made to develop a satisfactory dark-blue strain.

The outer coat of the Viennese Rabbit should be soft and dense and glossy, not less than 1¼" long. The undercoat, also thick and even, should be about ⅝" long. For the outer color, a deep, dark, shiny blue is wanted; it should penetrate as deeply to the skin as possible. The blue of the undercolor may be somewhat lighter.

Other color varieties of the Viennese Rabbit developed in Europe. One is the black, with jet-black surface color and blue undercoat; its physical features are the same as those of the blue, listed above. There is also a gray, somewhat smaller than the blue, its average weight being about nine pounds; its color is a dark-gray. Finally, white Viennese, weighing about ten pounds and resembling the blues in type and form, have been produced. Their eyes are blue. They are not related to the blue variety.

The young of the Viennese Rabbit are born with their natural color. The litters can be culled on the third day, so that youngsters with the lightest color may be discarded. It requires from seven to twelve months for the fur to reach its top condition.

Marilyn Albaugh, with one of her top-prize winners at Tuscarawas County Fair

Marilyn and Nancy Albaugh, with two of their finest prize winners at Tuscarawas County Fair

Photos by James W. Albaugh

Photo by The Harmons through courtesy of Ernie Gibbs

Close-up view of row of rabbit cages taken at the M & H Ranch, Ft. Myers, Florida, which is operated by Mr. and Mrs. Melvin W. Birkren. The ranch has two buildings, each 150 feet long; they house approximately 800 rabbits, mainly Californians.

Rabbit fur plays an important role in today's fashion. TO RIGHT: A capelet of natural rabbit that has a chinchilla coloring. BELOW: A natural sheared white rabbit jacket.

Photographs from
Harold J. Rubin Furs

Helmut Scheide

ABOVE: Chinchilla buck, small type. Special honor award winner
BELOW: Giant Chinchilla, doe. Scored 96 points in show and was
awarded top prize

C. Misset Verlag

C. Misset Verlag

Belgian Hare

Beveren doe

Helmut Scheide

C. Misset Verlag

Angora

Typical example of utility Californians kept at M & H Ranch, Ft. Myers, Fla.

Photo by The Harmons through courtesy of Ernie Gibbs

ABOVE: German Giant doe. Top winner at exhibition, with 96 points.
BELOW: Harlequin (Japanese) buck. Top-prize winner, with 95 points.

Harlequin-colored Dutch rabbit

ABOVE: Havanna, doe. 95-point award winner. BELOW: Himalayan doe, awarded 95 points and special honor prize against heavy competition

J. Messner

ABOVE: Marburger Lilac (*Feh*), winner of special honor prize, with 95 points. BELOW: Dutch rabbit. Black doe.

C. Misset Verlag

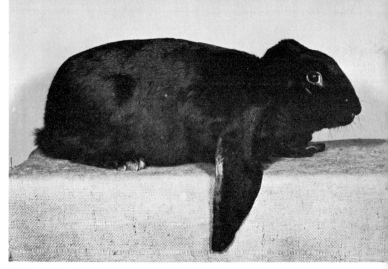

English Lopear, buck. Awarded 95 points and special prize

French Lopear

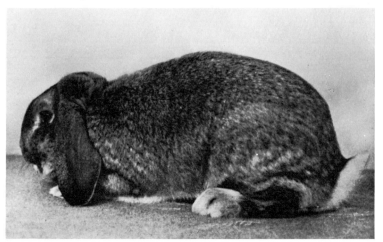

J. Messner

Helmut Scheide

C. Misset Verlag

ABOVE: Rex Chinchilla. This sizeable buck scored 95 points against strong competition.

LEFT AT TOP: Prize-winning Golden Palominos

LEFT AT CENTER: Polish Rabbit, doe. Scored 96 points at show

LEFT AT BOTTOM: Red New Zealand

Helmut Scheide

German Giant Silver, doe. Winner of top prize

Fox doe, 94-point show winner

Helmut Scheide

Marten

Siamese-colored Dwarf, buck.
Special-award winner

Helmut Scheide

Deutscher Kleintier Züchter and Helmut Scheide

Half-a-dozen Dwarf rabbits. From left to right: gray, black, Dutch, Himalayan, marten, and Siamese. Specially selected show exhibit

Dwarf Marten-brown buck.
94-point show winner

*Deutscher Kleintier Züchter
and Helmut Scheide*

C. Misset Verlag

Alaska

MONDET *Raymond* (RUSTICA)

Fauve-de Bourgogne (Yellow Burgundy). Popular, medium-heavy French breed

Helmut Scheide

Thuringian Chamois, doe. Winner of special honor award, with 95 points

Saxon-Gold. 95-point prize-winning buck

Helmut Scheide

MONDET *Raymond* (RUSTICA)

ABOVE: *Géant Papillon*, doe. First-prize winner at Rennes, France, 1962.
(Giant Butterfly or Checkered Giant). BELOW: German Weissgrannen
(white-tipped fur). This handsome buck won 94 points and special honor
prize against heavy competition

Helmut Scheide

Lux Buck. 95-point honor prize winner

Deutscher Kleintier Züchter

Lifting rabbits by ears or legs may injure them. With one hand take hold of a fold of skin over shoulder, then use other hand to support weight of the hindquarters.

Photo by The Harmons through courtesy of Ernie Gibbs

Doe with litter—excellent utility stock of Californian breed. Photographed at M & H Ranch, Ft. Myers, Florida, which is operated by Mr. and Mrs. Melvin W. Birkren

PEDIGREE

No. _____

Sold to _____

Address _____

Date _____

Sex _____

Born _____

Ear No. _____

Name _____

Reg. No. _____

Col. _____ Wt. _____

Ear No. _____

Sire _____
Reg. No. _____
Col. _____ Wt. _____
Ear No. _____

Breed _____

Dam _____
Reg. No. _____
Col. _____ Wt. _____
Ear No. _____

Sire _____
Reg. No. _____
Col. _____ Wt. _____
Ear No. _____

Dam _____
Reg. No. _____
Col. _____ Wt. _____
Ear No. _____

Sire _____
Reg. No. _____
Col. _____ Wt. _____
Ear No. _____

Dam _____
Reg. No. _____
Col. _____ Wt. _____
Ear No. _____

Sire _____
Reg. No. _____
Col. _____ Wt. _____
Ear No. _____
Dam _____
Reg. No. _____
Col. _____ Wt. _____
Ear No. _____

Sire _____
Reg. No. _____
Col. _____ Wt. _____
Ear No. _____
Dam _____
Reg. No. _____
Col. _____ Wt. _____
Ear No. _____

Sire _____
Reg. No. _____
Col. _____ Wt. _____
Ear No. _____
Dam _____
Reg. No. _____
Col. _____ Wt. _____
Ear No. _____

Sire _____
Reg. No. _____
Col. _____ Wt. _____
Ear No. _____
Dam _____
Reg. No. _____
Col. _____ Wt. _____
Ear No. _____

I hereby certify that this PEDIGREE is correct
to the best of my knowledge and belief.

Signed _____

Address _____

(See reverse side for show winnings)

SUPPLIED BY ALUMINUM MARKER WORKS, BEAVER FALLS, PA.

CERTIFICATE OF BREEDING

I hereby certify that I have this day bred _____ to _____
(Dam)   (Sire)

No. _____

Sold to _____

Address _____

Date _____

Born _____

Ear No. _____

Pedigree of prospective young

Of _____

Sire _____
Reg. No. _____
Col. _____ Wt. _____
Ear No. _____

Breed _____

Dam _____
Reg. No. _____
Col. _____ Wt. _____
Ear No. _____

Sire _____
Reg. No. _____
Col. _____ Wt. _____
Ear No. _____

Dam _____
Reg. No. _____
Col. _____ Wt. _____
Ear No. _____

Sire _____
Reg. No. _____
Col. _____ Wt. _____
Ear No. _____

Dam _____
Reg. No. _____
Col. _____ Wt. _____
Ear No. _____

Sire _____
Reg. No. _____
Col. _____ Wt. _____
Ear No. _____
Dam _____
Reg. No. _____
Col. _____ Wt. _____
Ear No. _____

Sire _____
Reg. No. _____
Col. _____ Wt. _____
Ear No. _____
Dam _____
Reg. No. _____
Col. _____ Wt. _____
Ear No. _____

Sire _____
Reg. No. _____
Col. _____ Wt. _____
Ear No. _____
Dam _____
Reg. No. _____
Col. _____ Wt. _____
Ear No. _____

Sire _____
Reg. No. _____
Col. _____ Wt. _____
Ear No. _____
Dam _____
Reg. No. _____
Col. _____ Wt. _____
Ear No. _____

I hereby certify that this CERTIFICATE is
correct to the best of my knowledge and belief

Signed _____

Address _____

(See reverse side for show winnings)

SUPPLIED BY ALUMINUM MARKER WORKS, BEAVER FALLS, PA.

All forms by courtesy of Aluminum Marker Works, Beaver Falls, Pa.

STUD RECORD CARD

Name of Buck _____

Date Born_____ Tag No._____ Hutch No._____

NAME OF DOES SERVED	Date Served	Date Tested	No. of Young

STOCK RECORD

LITTER	SIRE	DAM	STRAIN	BORN
NO.	NO.	NO.	NO.	

MALES NOS. { } HUTCH NO._____

FEMALE

BREEDING RECORD

No. _____ NAME _____ STRAIN _____

SERVED BY	Date Served	Date Tested	Date Born	No. of Young	Litter No.	No. Weaned

FOR _____

From _____

BREEDERS AND SHIPPERS OF

HIGH GRADE RABBITS

Town_____ State_____

Production records and vital statistics are a necessity for all persons who keep rabbits, be it for pleasure or profit. The forms above are typical of the sort used by well organized breeders.

Deutscher Kleintier Züchter

Angora rabbit-breeding farm

Exterior view of M & H Rabbit Ranch Building at Fort Myers, Florida

Photo by The Harmons through courtesy of Ernie Gibbs

Interior view of M & H Rabbit Ranch building. Note the wide aisle, the feed-hoppers, lighting, and ventilating equipment. The ranch houses approximately 800 rabbits. Weekly output of dressed rabbit meat is about 150 lbs. Does are bred four times a year. Each week about 100 young are born

Photo by The Harmons through courtesy of Ernie Gibbs

Three-tier Stock Hutch suitable for use indoors or outdoors. It is 5 ft. long x 4½ ft. high x 2 ft. wide; 6 compartments. Also available 6 ft. long x 4 ft. high x 2 ft. wide. *Courtesy Hylyne Rabbit Appliances, Northwich, Cheshire*

The "Royal" Hutch, outdoor model. Movable litter boards and drop-in doors. Non-spill water trough can be filled from outside. 4 ft. deep x 2 ft. wide x 22" at front, 19" at back. *Hylyne Rabbit Appliances.*

General purpose rabbit cage. Stainless steel. Door, back, top, and sides perforated. Door equipped with magnetic catch, door pull, and card holder. 18" wide x 18⅛" deep x 14½" high. Reprinted from *Animal Care Equipment* (March, 1965), issued by the National Institutes of Health, Washington, D.C.

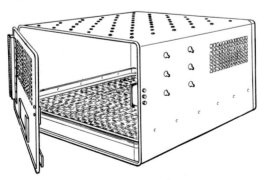

All photographs on these pages from Deutcher Kleintier Züchter

Walls and bottoms of these hutches are covered with special plastic material, which is warmer than ordinary wood, and which cannot be soiled by the rabbits

Outdoor ten-compartment hutch stocked with Viennese

Special three-tier battery used for both breeding and fattening

1. Feeder appropriate for leafy vegetables. Mounts on inside of cage door, or either side of cage. 11″ wide x 3½″ deep x 5″ high.

2. Feeder of wire-hanger type. Stainless steel. Mounts on inside of any cage that can accommodate 5″ spacing of the hangers. 4¾″ wide x 4½″ deep x 7⅞″ high. Both Nos. 1 and 2 above are from *Animal Care Equipment*, courtesy of the National Institutes of Health.

3. Creep-Feeder, fastened to hutch floor. Used for feeding special rations to bunnies after leaving nest. Doe cannot reach food or move feeder. *Courtesy Circle "K" Industries, Palatine, Illinois.*

4. Horizontal hay-rack. *Courtesy of Deutscher Kleintier Züchter.*

Outside metal feeder and water crock. This equipment is adequate for the small hobbyist. *Photo by Art Ammon*

1.

2.

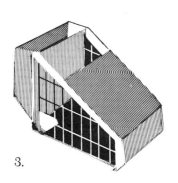

3.

4.

Automatic watering system provides even flow of fresh water at all times.

Cage battery equipped with automatic feeders. Note ample space between upper and lower tiers; also slanting dirt-catcher below top tier.

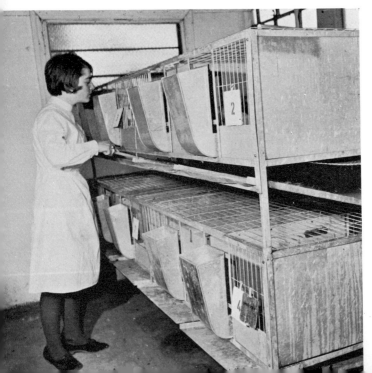

Outside racks for handy feeding
of greens

Inner view of rabbit shipping box

Deutscher Kleintier Züchter

Photos from Deutscher Kleintier Züchter

BELOW: The hundreds of exhibition cages shown below are in a hall which
houses major competitive shows in Stuttgart, Germany

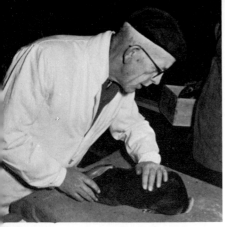

Judge at show, examining rabbit

Deutscher Kleintier Züchter

Group of judges at work

Deutscher Kleintier Züchter

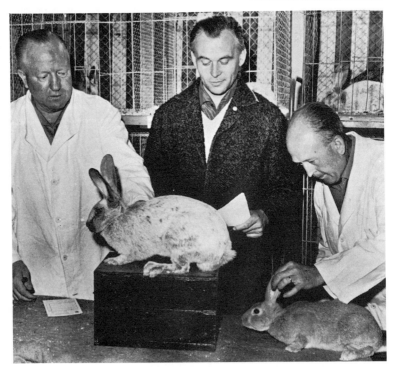

Toy Rabbits

Toy Rabbits are a Dutch development. They were first exhibited in 1938 in Haarlem. Of the fourteen shown, ten were gray, three blue, and one black-silver. In 1964, Toy Lop-ears appeared for the first time at several Dutch shows.

Today Toy Rabbits are favorites with many fanciers, not only in Holland, but also in Germany and other European countries. Wherever lack of maintenance facilities, as in most modern towns and cities, and high feed costs pose a real problem to keeping rabbits, Toy Rabbits provide the solution. Young fanciers especially like small rabbits, since they require but little space to keep in sound health and, of course, much less feed than the large breeds.

Apparently, the reduction of size and weight in Toys— they weigh only about three or four pounds—has affected their fertility, the litters being usually small. Moreover, during the first few hours following birth, the young Toys require extra warm nests, else they may not survive. In order to assure litters of vigorous Toys, it is imperative that only truly robust and normal animals be used for breeding.

SOME FOREIGN VARIETIES

Of the numerous breeds of domestic rabbits kept in various European countries, the following have been selected as being more or less typical representatives.

Alaska

A medium-sized crossbreed, originated in Germany in 1907, its glossy, jet-black fur to resemble that of the Alaskan fox; hence the name "Alaska."

Perlfeh

(Pearl Siberian Squirrel)

A small, very handsome, blue-gray rabbit, established in 1936 in Germany. Light-gray hairs with dark tips, sharply defined, represent the "pearling," which should be small and fine, and cover the entire body evenly. The coat is to resemble the pearly coat of the *Feh*, the Siberian squirrel.

Thuringian Rabbit

This variety was formerly called Chamois Thuringian (*Gemsfarbig*). It is one of the hardiest and best-developed breeds. Its body is compact; its normal weight is about eight pounds. The yellow-brown surface color is shot with dark-brown guard-hairs. The head has a dark mask. The young attain mature coloration at the age of eight months. This very handsome rabbit is especially popular in Holland and Switzerland.

Checkered German Giant

With a body length of at least twenty-five inches, and a normal weight of thirteen pounds, this well-marked rabbit is valued as an excellent meat and pelt producer. Two litters per year, with five or six young, are recommended for this giant breed. It is raised in two colors—black-and-white, and blue-and-white. The Checkered German Giant Rabbit is a favorite with many breeders in almost all European countries.

Yellow Burgundy

As a typical French product, *Fauve de Bourgogne,* a medium-sized rabbit, weighing about nine pounds, may be cited. Its yellow, lion-colored fur is long and dense. The thick undercoat is white at the base. There are conspicuous eye-circles. The breed is a great favorite with French fanciers.

White Hotot

Named after Hotot-en-Ange, the French locality where this variety was produced from various white-checkered rabbits, the White Hotot is of medium size. It is wholly white, except for narrow, black circles around the dark-brown eyes —a very striking and very old fancy variety. It has a fairly long, dense fur, with a thick undercoat.

CHAPTER FOUR

Essentials of Breeding and of Raising Young

Stud Buck
Breeding Doe
Importance of Record-Keeping
Nest Control
Keeping Foster Does
Litter Size
Weaning the Litter
Methods of Breeding

S UCCESS in raising any kind of livestock is largely dependent on the selection and the proper maintenance of the right sort of breeding animals, on the intelligent application of suitable methods of breeding, and on the proper care of the young. Success in raising domestic rabbits holds no exception to this general rule. Whether beginner or experienced hand, the reader is urged to note carefully the fundamental suggestions relating to the important aspects of breeding and raising young offered in the following pages, based as these are on extensive practical experience. Of all the chapters in this book, this one should be to him the most meaningful, useful, and helpful. As such, he would do well to read it over several times.

Rabbits to be bred should be healthy and vigorous, fully

developed, of good ancestry, and conform as much as possible to the standard of perfection of their particular breed, especially if they are meant for exhibition purposes. Those belonging to the large varieties are bred when they are approximately nine months old, while the medium-large varieties are bred at eight months, and the small ones at seven months. One should not forget, however, that age is by no means so determining a factor for breeding fitness as is the physical condition of the individual animal.

Stud Buck

First of all, the stud buck should meet the standard requirements of his breed in as many qualities as possible. In general, he should appear as vigorous and masculine as possible. He has a larger head, a wider breast, stronger muscles, and thicker skin than the doe. His eye is lively, his temperament keen. He is full of vitality, thus likely to produce fertile and hardy young. Listless or fat bucks should not be used for breeding. The stud buck's undercoat should be dense. Color and markings of fur should be typical of his breed. Wherever possible, it is wise to examine the buck's inheritance over several generations: the various litters will reveal hidden qualities, both good and bad, not visible in the buck's outer appearance. First-prize winners do not necessarily make good stud bucks, since they may be the accidental products of inferior parents.

Male rabbits are sexually mature at the age of four to five months. Ordinarily, one buck is sufficient for mating ten does. Regular, neither too little nor too much, use of the stud buck is advisable. At first, a young, fully developed buck is used only every fourteen days, the use then being gradually increased to three times weekly, with five times the maximum number. He should not be used while molting or immediately after feeding. The best time is before feeding early morning or evening. In some instances, bucks are used three times a day, with due allowance for suitable intervals. It has been found that more does than bucks appear in litters sired by bucks at short intervals.

Young stud bucks should be treated gently to avoid their getting angry and so becoming difficult to handle. It is best to keep them separately at the age of eight weeks in hutches that afford them plenty of room for exercise and normal development. They should be able neither to see nor to smell their kind, else they get too excited. Needless to say, they should be fed well, but not too well, to avoid their getting fat and listless.

Stud bucks which produce desirable offspring should be kept as long as possible. The more litters their keeper gets from them, the more he learns about their ability to transmit desirable and not so desirable qualities to their offspring. Of course, a stud buck's usefulness varies: with some of them, it lessens noticeably after three years, while others may produce sound young when they are six or more years old. Since a buck's offspring over a period of time—there may be as many as one hundred and eighty young in one year from one buck—are far more numerous than a doe's, he transfers his good and bad traits to many more young than does a doe; hence his greater importance in the breeding scheme.

Breeding Doe

To serve as an effective breeder, a doe should be in excellent physical condition, well-developed, but not fat, and have, so far as the special variety of which she is a member is concerned, as many desirable traits as possible. In this connection it is wise to compare her point by point with the ideal of the official standard, especially if she belongs to a fancy variety and is to produce exhibition-quality young. If according to the standard she has major faults, she is quite likely to transmit them to her offspring; so there is no use keeping her. If she is young and a likely show prospect according to the standard, it is well to scrutinize available production records of her parents and grandparents to ascertain just what quality offspring they have produced. Such records, if kept properly, should reveal not only the good points of each animal, but also the inferior points, against which the breeder must guard so as not to emphasize them in any way in his breedings.

Domestic rabbits have a gestation period of thirty-one days. They are very prolific, raising as many as three, and up to five, litters a year, the young being weaned when they are six weeks old. Does are usually bred when they are eight months old.

A doe gives unmistakable signs when she is in heat, that is, ready for breeding. Instead of sitting still, she will be hopping about restlessly in her hutch, rubbing her head against the sides of it. At this time, her external sex organs are enlarged and bright red. (A pale, dry vagina is almost a sure sign that the doe is not receptive.) Incidentally, before mating her, it is well to examine them to make sure there is no infection likely to be transferred to the buck. The most favorable time for breeding her is early morning or evening, before feeding. For this purpose she is placed in the hutch of the buck. Under no condition should the buck be placed in her hutch, where she would at once attack him. Mating usually takes place within a few minutes and is complete when the buck falls over on his side. The doe is then promptly returned to her hutch. About ten days later, she may be returned to the buck's hutch for testing. If she makes frightening noises, fights him, and otherwise refuses to accept him, she is in all probability pregnant. Pseudo-pregnancy is a 16–

18-day period during which the doe cannot conceive. It may result from either sterile coitus, or from being jumped by another doe. If there is nesting activity by the doe, such as pulling wool, within 16 to 20 days of mating, it certainly points to pseudo-pregnancy. She should be promptly placed with the buck, daily if necessary, until a mating has been effected. Does kept together should be separated within three weeks of being mated.

During pregnancy the doe should be kept quiet, have good care and nourishing food. About fourteen days after mating, she will begin to chew up litter and move about restlessly in her hutch. Her milk teats will develop during pregnancy, their number varying between six and twelve. Frequently, there are eight teats, which suffice to furnish enough milk for six youngsters—a reasonable number to keep with the nursing mother. Toward the end of pregnancy the doe will finish building her nest, lining it with wool plucked from her body. A week before she kindles, it is well to provide her with a clean nestbox and fresh nesting material, such as hay or straw. Also she should have access to cool water all day long, and especially so during the warm summer months. Most litters are born during the night. They are warmly bedded in a woolly nest, built either in a box or in a corner of the hutch. A doe should never be disturbed while kindling.

A doe which has raised sizable litters of good quality over a period of three or more years, thus showing excellent production, should by all means be kept as long as she maintains a satisfactory production rate. She represents truly valuable capital to her owner. And it is always much more satisfactory to keep proven breeders than to run risks with young, unproven does. Of course, if a doe's litters contain too many weak, mismarked, or otherwise unsatisfactory young, then she is best discarded. Incidentally, it is well to remember that the building of a sound strain or family of rabbits is greatly affected by the age of the individual members. The older these are, the more reliable the offspring, because so much more is known about the does and bucks.

Some novices forget that the outer appearance of a breeding rabbit is no reliable indicator of its hidden, inherited traits. Only after a number of litters have been produced and have matured can one tell if his choice was correct, or reasonably so. The more specific information about the breeding rabbit's ancestry the fancier has, or can obtain, the more likely is he to make an intelligent choice. A hasty selection based mainly on outer appearance or on insufficient experimentation is of no value. Only judging based on as large a number of litters as possible is likely to be satisfactory. In this connection it is well to emphasize that no breeding scheme can produce traits or qualities in the offspring which were not present in the ancestors. The best a fancier can do is to select his breeders in accordance with their inheritance.

Importance of Record-Keeping

The man or woman who keeps rabbits for a definite purpose, be that pleasure or profit, or both, cannot possibly remember the multitude of details involved in keeping track of important production and other vital information that is to serve as guide to future operations. The practical solution to this common problem is keeping records. Far too many rabbit fanciers fail to keep any records at all; they are shocked when their stock fails to win at the shows, where usually they have to compete with exhibitors who do keep records. Ordinarily, it is well to begin record-keeping with the young rabbits, noting characteristics of form, fur, color, markings, feed consumption, rate of growth, fertility, and other essential data, to serve both as future identification and as reliable guides to the animals' use for breeding, exhibition, etc. Naturally, the nature and the extent of the information written down are based on the fancier's need and his probable future use for it. He may simply keep a card record on each rabbit, thus assembling in due time a convenient and valuable card file. The more concisely he writes the desired information on each card, using abbreviations, etc., the less time it takes to keep the system in useful operation. Instead of assembling the cards in a file, the breeder may wish to attach a card to each hutch, giving hutch number; name of rabbit; tattoo number or other positive identification; date of birth; sire; dam; mating date; if a doe, mated by such and such a buck; results; and brief miscellaneous notes.

Records kept usually fall into more or less well-defined groups: those pertaining to costs of operation, listing the various expenditures; those pertaining to management and maintenance, listing all items pertaining to breeding, infertility, mortality, etc., a good deal of which information may be gleaned from the individual hutch cards. Finally, records may be kept relating to the selection of future breeding stock, listing the breeding efficiency of each rabbit, including mating results, proportion of bucks and does in each litter, milk yield of a doe (measured indirectly by the weight of the litter at three weeks of age), growth rates of young and their resistance to disease.

The breeder should suit his recording system to his own special needs. If he keeps Angoras, he will record the wool yield, its quality and amount at each clipping, in addition to such other information as he thinks helpful in the over-all operation of his rabbitry. If he markets meat rabbits, he will want to keep track of dressing-out percentages for the various carcasses, thus to determine which strain or strains of rabbits furnish the better quality of carcasses. He will want to know also the quantity of feed necessary to produce carcasses of a given weight. In sum, each breeder's records should be designed to answer those questions specifically, the answers to which will enable him to improve the operation and management of his particular enterprise; hence the desirability for each breeder to keep individualized records, based on his own specific needs.

Nest Control

Nest control concerns the number and the condition of the young in the nest. When this writer kept rabbits as a boy, a good many years ago, opening the nest for inspection was frowned upon by the rabbit fancy in general. He simply waited—rather impatiently and excitedly—for the shy little bunnies to emerge reluctantly from their nestbox when they were between three and four weeks old. Today's practice favors nest control within 24 hours after kindling. The doe is placed in another hutch, but not a buck's, during inspection of the nest. In order to lift her, the loose skin of the back over the shoulders is grasped in one hand, while the other hand supports the hindquarters; she is then held in one's arms. Where nestboxes are used, the does are left in their hutches and the boxes are taken out. The nest is opened carefully. First, the young are counted, then examined as to their physical condition. Runts and weaklings are promptly eliminated. Dead young are rarely found in the nest, since the doe will usually remove them from the nest after kindling. Should the young perchance be scattered over the floor of the hutch, they are collected and returned to the nest, while their mother is out of the hutch. If the youngsters are cold, they must be warmed first. Should the entire litter be lost, the doe can be mated again the following day, when she will usually accept service quite readily. When the doe is returned to her hutch following nest control, she will want to go at once to her nest. Her attention is best distracted by giving her some tidbit, such as a carrot or some greens. After fifteen or twenty minutes, the young in the nest will have lost the smell of the fancier's hands, so the doe will accept them without trouble.

The young rabbits in the nest should appear plump, full of milk, and they should be lying still. If they are restless, it is usually a sign of insufficient nursing. At any rate, after control the young are put carefully back in the nest so that they lie nicely side by side; then they are covered with wool and finally with some hay or straw. They will be somewhat restless, since their individual places in the nest have been changed during control. The doe should not be returned to the hutch until the babies are quiet. Moreover, control must not last long since the entirely naked and blind young need warmth more than anything else.

Nest control is best continued after the first day. If at any time, thin and undernourished young are found in the nest, then some will have to be taken away and the doe be given more milk-producing feed. There is quite a difference in nursing does: some will raise six or more young nicely, others but a few. The latter should be culled. Where a number of breeding does are kept, they may be mated at the same time so that, if need be, litters may be evened up. When transferring young from nest to nest, the does are taken out of their hutches for half an hour or so. By that time the transferred young will have taken on the smell of their new nest, so that there will be no trouble from the doe.

Keeping Foster Does

Some fanciers with topnotch fancy does keep foster does, which should be of similar size. These are mated the same day as the fancy does. If they are proven breeders and good nursing mothers, their use may be practical. It can happen, of course, that a fancy doe will throw a large litter and the foster doe none at all, or vice versa. The best practice is to mate a number of does on the same day, then to even up the litters, if need be. This should be done only after several days when the milk flow is in full swing. The transferred young are best placed in the middle among the others so that all will soon smell alike. The doe should be kept out of her hutch for half an hour; when replaced, she should be given some tidbit to distract her attention from the nest.

Size of Litter

The number of teats which the nursing doe has determines the maximum number of young to be raised by her. If the youngsters have to fight for places at the teats, they are not likely to get sufficient milk. If too many young are left with the mother, they are almost always hungry and will leave the nest too soon in order to seek food. In this way, weaklings develop poorly and die sooner or later. On the other hand, too few nursing young are not economical. There are no hard and fast rules that can be followed so far as the number of young to be left with their mother is concerned. The breeder should know the capacity of his does.

Early sexing of the young rabbits is done by placing a youngster in your left hand and on its back. Pull the little tail back and you will note two openings—the anus and the sexual part. The distance between them is different in some youngsters. If both openings are close together, then the youngster is a doe; if farther apart, then it is a buck. The sexing is best done at the first nest control, since differences disappear after a few days. Then sexing is possible only at the age of six weeks or so.

Rabbits, as against hares, are born blind and naked. When they are ten days old, their eyes open. Should they remain closed, then they should be washed with warm water. At this time, the nestbox is taken out and thoroughly cleaned. As soon as the young rabbits, which stay in the nest from three to four weeks, begin to eat, their ration is increased. The nursing period normally lasts from eight to ten weeks. Youngsters less than eight weeks of age should not be weaned, or only when they are very husky. The young may nurse until they are four months old; a long nursing period is conducive to growth and development. Of course, such a long period is not practical in cases in which the doe must be bred again.

It is necessary to give a nursing doe and her litter ample room, so that there will be no crowding when the young leave the nest. Crowding makes for poor development, and it increases the danger of sickness, especially if there is a large accumulation of droppings. The hutch should be cleaned out at least once a week. Where wire bottoms are used, the danger of infection is greatly lessened.

Weaning the Litter

In order to prevent a concentration of milk in the nursing doe, it is best not to wean all young at one time. First, wean the strongest youngsters, then the weaker ones. If there is sufficient room and the young can be kept separately, they will grow better and faster. The young may be kept together, if need be, but not the bucks. If these are castrated, it should be done at the age of four months or so, for then they will get along with one another until they are ready for butchering. Where runs are used for the weaned young rabbits, they should be at least 5' x 20' to accommodate between fifteen and twenty animals.

Before weaning the young, it is often advisable to mark them so that later they may be correctly identified. Without suitable identification, there can be no effective breed control. Tattoo marks consisting of letters or numbers, or both, are placed in the inner surface of the rabbit's ear by means of an electric tattoo needle or other special instrument obtainable at rabbit supply houses. Does are marked in the right ear, bucks in the left ear.

Feeding young rabbits after weaning should be done with care. Healthy young are lively: they come to the front of the hutch at feeding time. They are fed three times daily, being given only so much feed as they will clean up in fifteen minutes. Fresh, clean green food should form an important part of their diet. In addition, they should have good-quality hay before them at all times. After meals all food leftovers should be promptly removed. If the youngsters' droppings are too soft, or if other digestive disturbances seem evident, a first-class leafy hay will often serve as an effective corrective. Litters born in the spring of the year usually develop the fastest, hence are most satisfactory.

The aim in raising young rabbits is to produce animals with ample meat and good fur. Especially in utility breeds, a compact, stocky body is wanted, with body breadth and torso depth each about one-third of body length. Bodily shape and form affect production capacity very much, favorably or otherwise; for this reason, attention to form and shape in young rabbits is very much worth while.

Young rabbits with weak heads, thin, poorly furred ears, long, narrow bodies, and thin, long legs are usually poor prospects. They should be disposed of at the first opportunity. In good litters, all members should grow up equally well. An examination of the youngsters' fur will reveal noticeable differences: some will have a good, medium-long fur; others a shorter fur. Specimens with either too long or too short fur are unsuited for breeding. Most breed standards demand a thick, half-long fur with a dense undercoat. The top hair should be well distributed over the body and should be neither too soft nor too stiff or hard. When the fur is stroked against the growth, it should show a certain amount of resistance. Density of fur is far more important than length. When the youngsters reach the age of three months, they discard the nest-hairs so that proper judging of their fur becomes more possible.

Methods of Breeding

There are various methods or systems of breeding rabbits, with the scientific in all probability being used the least by the average rabbit-keeper. To serve even as a fairly reliable guide to efficient present and future breeding procedures, nearly all of them require detailed, conscientious record-keeping, not just for a few months or even a year or two, but as long as the rabbitry is in purposeful operation. Unless the records kept are up-to-date and complete, a task requiring continual time and effort, their value as reasonably accurate interpreters of current methods, and as reasonably dependable guides to satisfactory future operations, is, to put it mildly, doubtful.

It is true that the great majority of rabbit-keepers in this country make little or no attempt to record their breeding and other important operations, that they regard such work as an unnecessary and most inconvenient interference with the enjoyment of their hobby or the conduct of their business. For this reason, this writer has refrained from discussing detailed, scientific breeding systems applicable to modern rabbit culture. Another, and perhaps even more relevant reason is the lack of scientific knowledge and training possessed by the average rabbit fancier. If the reader wishes to apply the laws of inheritance and related topics, he can obtain a grasp of practical essentials by studying genetics.

Any school or public library will lend him authentic, up-to-date books on genetics and related subjects.

As is true of any hobby or business dealing with livestock, its participants fall into many diversified groups. When it comes to keeping domestic rabbits, there is the pet-lover, young or old, man or woman, who at home cares for a given number of these amiable, noiseless creatures simply because he or she likes them. Then, there is the backyard hobbyist, whose small herd is kept to yield enjoyment and relaxation, and some profit. Often he is a retired worker, a pensioner, who wants something "alive" to keep mind and body occupied, for he has much leisure time on his hands. So he keeps some rabbits, whose daily maintenance helps him to fill otherwise idle hours with enjoyable, purposeful activity. There is also the dyed-in-the-wool breeder, a genuine fancier, who would not be without rabbits under any conditions. His devotion to them is founded on deep interest in breed individuality, and on a profound liking for them. He is the expert, who can "talk rabbits"—mainly *his* rabbits—all day long to anyone willing to listen. Finally, there is the operator of the commercial rabbitry, a business keeping hundreds of breeding does for the sole purpose of producing a marketable, profitable carcass and pelt in large quantities. His liking for rabbits is based almost solely on their productivity.

Of the above-mentioned devotees to rabbit culture, few make a concerted effort to interest themselves seriously in so-called systems of breeding, that is, applying a certain one thoroughly and unvaryingly over a period of years, and, what is absolutely essential, at the same time write down their day-to-day findings completely and conscientiously. Among these few would doubtless be the true fancier who keeps a herd of high-quality rabbits for show purposes, and the commercial breeder, whose dependence on daily cost, maintenance, and production figures compels him to keep books if he wants to stay in business. So the aim of the one is to raise top-quality exhibition animals, at least a few first- or second-prize winners each season, in order to keep his prestige as a successful fancier intact. The aim of the other, specifically, is to increase the dollars-and-cents income from his herd by raising larger litters, faster-growing young, better-quality pelts, etc.

In purposeful breeding of domestic rabbits, selection and elimination are the key factors likely to lead to success. Selection of the right breeding stock is mainly dependent on the skill of the breeder, especially on his knowledge and understanding of the varieties he keeps. Selection is made on the strength of both outer appearance and the important details, favorable and unfavorable, furnished by the pedigree. To be of value, this document should contain details of *all* ancestors. The name of each rabbit should be accompanied by specific characteristics and particular performances. The pedigree will serve as a practical aid to selection only if it provides unbiased, correctly compiled details.

Elimination, the other key factor in successful breeding, is applied to all rabbits which for any good reason are undesirable. Certainly, those afflicted with major faults should be promptly culled. A breeder should not let sentiment interfere when it comes to ridding his herd of animals which do not meet the breed standard of perfection in one or more major qualities. The sum and substance of livestock improvement lies in the concentration of favorable qualities and in the elimination of unfavorable qualities.

A rabbit's qualities or traits are the result of inheritance as well as of environment; hence to strengthen or to increase them, there must be improvement of inheritance or of environment, or both. The rabbit breeder is indeed fortunate in that he can to a large degree control the environment of his animals, as by means of better housing, feeding, and management in general. He can thus better their health, increase their size, their milk yield, their fur quality, and numerous other desirable traits, the improvement lasting usually only for the life of the particular animal. To pass improvements on to future generations, various methods of genetical change may be applied.

There is, first of all, *inbreeding*, by means of which closely related members of the same family, as brother to sister or parent to offspring, are paired up. Continued for twenty or more generations, this method will result in genetic uniformity. If bad qualities are present in the stock when inbreeding is first begun, they will soon appear in the offspring, which must then be severely culled. Inbreeding can make the best only of *existing* qualities. It cannot contribute new ones. However, if very careful selection is exercised, inbreeding will fix desirable dominant and recessive qualities, thus tending toward uniformity. In the hands of a skillful, experienced breeder this method will prove progressively resultful.

For most rabbit fanciers, *linebreeding*, a less concentrated system of inbreeding, is useful. It provides for the pairing of more distantly related members of the same strain. Thus, it may consist of mating descendants back to a desirable buck, say, a champion, for a number of generations to produce an inbred family. It implies breeding along a certain line or direction, as, for instance, coupling cousin with cousin, or uncle with cousin, aunt with nephew, and so on. By mating more distant relatives one with another, the danger of degeneration supposedly attending close inbreeding, such as a brother-and-sister mating, is presumably averted.

Whenever a rabbit breeder wishes to inject new blood into his strain, he resorts to *outcrossing*. For this purpose he carefully selects a buck from the herd of another fancier, whose strain he thinks will blend smoothly with his own. The mixing of two different bloodlines may result in quality offspring in the first generation, at the same time increasing undesirable variations, which may crop up in future generations. Careless crossing indulged in by the inexperienced breeder who buys a buck here and a doe there without knowing their ancestry or their progeny will produce such a mixture of physical and mental traits in the offspring as to make it impossible for their owner to establish any uniformity among them. Incidentally, careful, highly selective crossbreeding has produced most of our modern breeds of domestic rabbits.

CHAPTER FIVE

Housing and Maintenance

Location of Rabbitry
Hutches
Earthworms
Shelters
Nestboxes
Feeding Utensils
Watering Equipment

WHEN deciding on a suitable location for a rabbitry, even a modest one, the important thing to do first of all is to find out if there are any local ordinances or other legal restrictions likely to interfere with rabbit-keeping. The fairly recent population "explosion" has changed considerably the building and sanitation regulations in many localities which formerly permitted various livestock keeping on a fairly generous scale, but which now prohibit it mainly on grounds of sanitation. In localities permitting rabbit-keeping as a hobby or as a part-time business, the number of animals which may be kept is definitely limited by ordinances. Moreover, their maintenance is subject to more or less regular inspection by representatives of the local health department, who usually exercise strict supervision over such and similar livestock projects. Thus, if rabbits are kept in overcrowded, smelly, or otherwise objectionable hutches, conditions often causing complaints from neighbors, the local health officer will demand prompt and permanent cleanup. In the light of the foregoing considerations, the prospective rabbit-keeper can save himself a deal of inconvenience, trouble, and money by making sure well *before* actually getting any rabbits that keeping them at or near his home will pose no special problem in complying readily with local laws, now or in the foreseeable future.

Location of Rabbitry

The proper location of a rabbitry is especially important if marketing is its principal purpose. This purpose is well served by a rabbit-raising community, already well organized for disposing of its products as profitably as possible. Moreover, the members of such a group usually concentrate on breeding a certain type or breed of rabbit, one which has proved profitable, in large numbers. At times a rabbit-raising community, acting like a "closed corporation," will not welcome the additional competition coming from a newly established rabbitry. At any rate, such a business should be located on fairly level, well-drained land, preferably sloping gently to the south and having as many shade trees as possible. There should, moreover, be sufficient additional land available to provide for any future expansion of the business.

When it comes to specific maintenance facilities, domestic rabbits by nature are not demanding. Like some other domestic animals, they will thrive if their hutches or other containers afford them ample light, fresh air, some sunshine, room for exercise, freedom from crowding, and clean floors. Being sensitive to climatic extremes, rabbits need protection against excessive summer heat and winter cold, direct drafts, windstorms, etc. In other words, all hutch equipment should be suited to the climatic conditions prevailing in the locality. Excessive heat and excessive cold, if not guarded against by means of proper equipment, will cause many deaths among rabbits.

Nowadays, domestic rabbits are kept by all manner of persons and under all sorts of conditions. At Easter time many young boys and girls receive so-called Easter bunnies as gifts, which they keep in makeshift cartons or cages that make thorough cleaning at best inconvenient and difficult; hence this important task is often put off and off, with disastrous effects on the rabbits. On the positive side, many boys and girls, as members of 4-H Clubs and classes in livestock keeping at public schools, are taught the principles and practices of modern rabbit culture very well. Thus, many a youngster's initial interest in keeping rabbits is stimulated to a degree at which it gradually results in the "making" of an intelligent and enthusiastic fancier.

Among the most unusual, and perhaps also the most economical, ways of keeping domestic rabbits with which this writer is familiar, are not hutch-keeping, colony-keeping, or similar sorts, but housing these gentle animals in the same stable with other domestic animals, principally goats and cows. In various sections of Europe the domestic rabbit was for many, many years, and still is, the workingman's regular meat supplier, and the goat his main milk supplier. Since both animals thrive on the same fare and similar care, what mode of keeping them could be more convenient, simple, and, above all, more economical than to house rabbits and goats together in the same stable? Neither animal bothered the other. The goats were tied up, so could not trample on the rabbits' nests, usually built in some corner of the stable. The latter lived largely on the greenstuff and the hay which the goats wasted and therefore rarely needed extra feed. Furthermore, the rabbits benefited from the regular stable cleaning and maintenance given the goats. But even well-to-do peasants and landowners, who kept cows in place of goats, found such rabbit-keeping satisfactory. There was always plenty of room in the straw-covered corners of the large, well-kept stable for the rabbits to build their nests safely. So accustomed to the presence of the rabbits were the cows, which were permanently stabled the year round, that losses among the rabbits were few and far between.

Hutches

There are various types of hutches from which to choose. The final selection depends on the owner's particular needs. His entire rabbitry may consist of only a few hutches or else of a spacious separate building housing many animals and carefully designed for future expansion. According to available space and the owner's convenience in servicing them, hutches are placed either indoors or outdoors.

Indoor hutches provide for both rabbits and their keeper protection from the weather. Moreover, temperatures indoors are much more easily controlled. And if he likes, the owner can breed his rabbits during the winter months. Since they are very accessible indoors, he can attend to their wants comfortably and conveniently. Among the drawbacks of using indoor hutches are the lack of sunshine, a certain amount of which every rabbit should have. Also rabbits kept indoors often lack dense coats. Rabbits kept in outdoor hutches, benefiting from the fresh air day and night, are usually healthier and more disease-resistant; they develop a better quality of fur. All hutches, it should be emphasized, whether placed indoors or outdoors, should be so designed and so constructed as to require a minimum of labor to service them promptly and thoroughly. They should preferably be portable so that they may be set in the shade in summer and in suitable shelter in winter.

There is a strong and encouraging tendency today to use all-metal hutches or wire cages. Not only do they facilitate feeding, watering, and cleaning, but they are easily disinfected, thus keeping the rabbits from getting diseases to which they might be subject if kept in the less sanitary wooden hutches. Moreover, the metal hutches rarely require repairs. While the initial investment in all-metal hutches or wire cages may loom large to the beginner, spread over years, the unit cost of these attractive, airy, clean, and practically indestructible hutches becomes quite reasonable. They are offered for sale in many sizes and models by rabbit-supply firms to suit small as well as large installations. The prospective user should write these firms for their illustrated catalogs, or, if possible, visit their display rooms to make his own personal inspection and selection. All in all, there is great satisfaction in knowing that one's rabbits are housed comfortably and cleanly, as in metal hutches or cages, where they may be maintained with a minimum of labor.

The *size* of the hutch should, of course, be suited to the size and weight of the rabbit it is meant to accommodate. Generally speaking, each breeding rabbit should have one square foot of floor space for each pound of mature live weight. An adult rabbit can be comfortable and raise young in a 2-by-6-foot hutch. Suitable hutch lengths are three feet for the smaller breeds, four feet for the medium-sized breeds, and from five to six feet for the larger ones. At least one-third of the hutch floor space should be reserved for the nestbox, which should be portable to provide additional floor space for the young at weaning time.

The *floor* of the hutch, which should slope slightly toward the rear for purposes of drainage, may be solid wood, part wood and part wire mesh, slat-wood, or wire mesh. The solid floor, covered with suitable bedding, is draft-proof and fairly easily cleaned. Moreover, it is cheaper than most other kinds. The partly solid floor is solid in the front of the hutch; in the rear it has a 6-to-8-foot strip of wire mesh. Slat floors are quite commonly used, the slats being one to two inches wide, one-half to three-quarters inch thick, placed at five-eighths-inch spacings. The wire-mesh floors, which are practically self-cleaning, aid in promoting disease prevention. They, as well as the partly solid and slat floors, may be mounted over a tray or sloping sheet of metal, where the droppings may be easily collected. Ordinarily, a 17-gauge hardware cloth, smooth and without projecting sharp points, is used, with half-inch mesh for all breeds. Joints may be kept free from rusting by having the metal flooring galvanized after welding.

Hutch doors should measure approximately 21" x 21". They should be large enough to allow for convenient handling of the rabbits, also for installing and removing nestboxes and other equipment. If feeding and watering can be done without opening doors, so much the better. To save labor, some doors are designed to cover a number of hutches. Usually hutch doors are hinged at the side to swing outward. They should be tight-fitting, easy to close, and be equipped with fasteners which the rabbits can't open. The wire on the door is fastened on the inside; otherwise the rabbits will gnaw the frame. The mesh should be fine enough to prevent mice and other unwelcome guests from entering the hutch. To prevent litter from falling out when the door is opened, a board is nailed in front of the door.

Varying with available space, hutches may be arranged in one, two, or three tiers. The one-tier setup is used a good deal, since neither stooping nor reaching is necessary at feeding or cleaning time. The two-tier arrangement, which makes for some saving in floors and roofs, should have the lower tier at least a foot or more off the floor, for purposes of ventilation and easy cleaning. Furthermore, between the roof of the lower hutch and the floor of the upper, there should be a clearance of six or more inches to allow for convenient cleaning. To avoid drippings from the upper hutch into the lower, the front of the latter should project five or six inches beyond the front of the upper. Three-tier installations are not often used, since the rabbits housed in the lower and in the upper tiers can be neither readily observed nor conveniently cared for. Wooden roofs covered with heavyweight roofing felt and sloping slightly to the rear for good drainage are economical and satisfactory.

Earthworms

Earthworms raised under hutches equipped with wire-mesh or other self-cleaning floors provide some additional income. The droppings are collected in wooden bins, which are about a foot deep and as wide and long as the hutch floors, in which earthworms are placed. For bedding, crushed or shredded leaves, rotted sawdust, rotted barnyard manure are used, in addition to the rabbit manure. These materials, thoroughly mixed together and watered, should furnish suitable bedding to a depth of from six to eight inches. They are watered and turned over each day for about a week, when they are ready to receive the worms, which are placed in a hole dug in the bedding and then covered up. The worm cultures should be kept moist, but not wet; they should not be disturbed for several weeks. Moreover, the surface of the bedding should occasionally be turned with a fork to keep it loose and airy. Ordinarily, worms will be ready for harvesting in about six or eight months after planting. The activity of the worms in the bins tends to prevent obnoxious odors from forming and flies from breeding in them. Many operators of rabbitries harvest quantities of earthworms year in and year out, thus adding appreciably to their income.

Shelters

Shelters meant for small or large rabbitries should be suited to climatic and other local conditions, and, of course, to the available capital. In their simplest form they may provide an open-front shed made of wood, with solid, sloping roof, back, and sides, as a protection against inclement weather. In regions enjoying mild climates, a lattice framework is often sufficient protection against strong, direct sunlight. Climbing roses and vines planted to cover this framework tend to furnish further shade and also to provide a natural setting. Such shelters, well lighted, may be equipped with lath shutters or durable curtains to exclude wind and rain.

More elaborate shelters, in the form of substantial, permanent buildings, involve the outlay of considerable money. Since they provide existing buildings for many years, they should be planned very carefully. Quite often already existing structures, such as poultry houses and livestock stables, can be effectively adapted to rabbit-housing, and at a great saving of money. In planning any permanent shelter, the foremost consideration should center on the saving of labor in every maintenance operation to be performed in the rabbitry. Automatic lighting, ventilating, heating, feeding, watering, and other labor-saving devices play a very important role in the efficient use of permanent shelters. To expedite cleaning, these shelters are commonly equipped with concrete, slightly sloping floors that can be easily and quickly washed down at any time.

Before the owner builds a more or less elaborate shelter for his rabbits, which may occupy large ground space, he should by all means familiarize himself with local building regulations. It will also be to his advantage to visit a number of local rabbit men to scrutinize their various installations as to suitable and successful housing equipment used in a particular locality. Such visits are bound to yield much practical information applicable to his own rabbit-housing problem, and thus to save him time, effort, and money.

Nestboxes

Nestboxes should be roomy enough to prevent crowding, yet small enough to keep the young rabbits warm. For medium-large breeds, a box 10" wide, 10" high, and 15" deep is quite suitable. These dimensions should, of course, be changed to suit small and large breeds. Apple and other boxes equipped with removable lids used for inspection, and with removable bottoms used for cleaning, may be used. Open top boxes do not conserve the much-needed warmth. At one end of the box should be the entrance hole, several inches from the bottom of the box; thus elevated, it may prevent youngsters being drawn from the nest when the doe jumps out of it. The entrance hole may take the form of a hinged door. The doe uses the top of the box to get away from her young when these have left the nest. Nail kegs of suitable size may also serve as nestboxes for rabbits. The open end of the nail keg may be covered up to one-third or one-half with a board extending some inches beyond the edge of the opening to prevent the "nestbox" from rolling. A few one-inch holes drilled in the rear end of the nail keg will furnish ventilation.

Additional protection against cold temperatures can be given the regular nestbox by simply setting it inside a larger box and by lining the intervening space on the sides with straw, newspapers, or other insulating material. The underside of the box-lid should also be covered with similar material. For purposes of ventilation a few small holes may be drilled in the box-lid. Insulating material may be placed also in the bottom of the nestbox to keep the young rabbits from making contact with the cold wood; this should be topped by a deep layer of fresh, clean straw into which the doe will burrow to make her nest.

Feeding Utensils

Feeding utensils are available at rabbit-supply and poultry-supply houses. The novice can save himself a great deal of time learning what kinds of equipment are necessary by simply calling at these business firms, which usually display the very latest in such wares. In selecting crocks and cans for feeding, he should give preference to glazed earthenware, heavy, non-tippable ones with lips that prevent the rabbits from scratching feed out. The crocks can be used for feeding whole grain or pellets. One-pound coffee cans, nailed to a heavy board, are also serviceable, even though they will rust in time. Individual feed hoppers, some of them equipped with three of four separate compartments in case the breeder wishes to feed different kinds of pellets or grains, are also in use. However, single-compartment hoppers are the most generally used, since most breeders feed only one kind of pellet. Most hoppers are provided with lids to prevent the rabbits from trying to jump into them. Many rabbit men make their own feed-hoppers from wood or other material; five-gallon cans can be made into inexpensive, lasting self-feeders.

For so-called creep-rations, special creep-feeders are used. They are designed to prevent mature animals from eating the creep-rations, while still allowing the youngsters ready access to them. Creep-feeders, obtainable at supply stores, are box-like metal containers, equipped with lids and fastened securely to the hutch floor. They are designed to give the young rabbits easy access to the special ration, at the same time preventing them from soiling it. For convenient filling, the lid can be opened with one hand, and for cleaning, the feeder can be readily removed from the cage.

Since rabbits are usually fed hay or green food, or both, hay mangers built into the hutches are useful. Both space and labor are saved by installing a V-shaped manger between two hutch units to serve both. Similarly shaped mangers, made of wood or sheet metal, are attached to the outside of the hutch. To save short pieces of hay or green food falling from the manger as the rabbits feed, a trough is placed underneath. It has a cover or guard to keep young rabbits from jumping into it and soiling the contents. The trough may be used also for feeding various supplemental grains.

Watering Equipment

Watering equipment is needful since the drinking requirements of domestic rabbits are rather high. Years ago when this writer kept rabbits in his boyhood days, it was generally believed that rabbits needed no drinking water, provided they were fed ample quantities of fresh, green food every day, including juicy root crops in winter. However, maintenance practices since that time have changed in many respects: today every rabbit kept in a hutch or a cage is given a full supply of fresh, clean drinking water, if need be, several times a day, as in the summertime. It is worth noting in this respect that the needs of livestock for water are over three times those for dry food. Young rabbits drink almost double the quantity of water drunk by adult rabbits. Nursing does, especially during the hot summer season, should be given fresh drinking water several times a day.

Watering utensils are of varied design. Commonly used

is the simple, non-tippable, glazed earthenware crock, four inches deep and eight inches in diameter, or the coffee can, nailed to a board or else to the wall of the hutch, both drinkers readily available and not expensive. Since their contents are subject to contamination, crocks and cans must be frequently cleaned.

Whenever the number of rabbits kept justifies the cash outlay, an automatic watering system provides numerous advantages. It does away with the laborious and time-consuming task of washing, disinfecting, and filling crocks and cans with fresh, clean water, thus saving much time and effort every single day. Moreover, the system is sanitary in that it tends to prevent the spread of disease by water. There is no difficulty in getting the rabbits, even the young just out of the nest, to drink from the automatic valves: they learn to do so quickly.

The commonly used automatic drinking system, available at rabbit-supply centers, has a break pressure tank equipped with a float valve, a one-half-inch supply pipe, a watering unit for each hutch, and valves. The last-mentioned serve to get rid of air bubbles, to drain the system when necessary, or to shut the water off entirely. Some rabbit men prefer to use one-gallon tanks in hot weather, since these get empty oftener, thus supplying fresh, clean water for the rabbits continuously. For the small breeds of rabbits, the water valve should be seven inches off the hutch floor, and for medium-large and large breeds it should be nine inches off the hutch floor. The pipe is installed on the outside at the rear of the hutches to prevent water from wetting the floor or the rabbits. A hole is cut in the rear of the hutch through which the rabbits use the valves. The watering system should be checked regularly to see that the valves function properly. It may happen that in unoccupied hutches valves not in use become clogged with mineral matter. When these hutches are again occupied, the valves should be examined for proper functioning. If the breeder is not prepared to install his own automatic watering system, he can usually get practical help from the supply houses, where, also, he can inspect any and all modern utensils and equipment used to supply water for domestic rabbits.

CHAPTER SIX

Feeding Rabbits

Factors Determining Food Consumption

A rabbit should be given food sufficient in nutritive content and in quantity to keep it in sound health and top production. Its individual requirements vary, first of all, with the breed to which it belongs. Naturally, the larger breeds eat much more than the smaller breeds. Other factors determining a rabbit's food consumption include age, i.e., whether young or mature; whether the function of the food is simply maintenance, as in dry does; or maintenance plus growth, as in does with nursing litters; or fattening of young or old animals. Climatic conditions also affect the amount of feed a rabbit will eat. In cold regions, it will necessarily require much more food in winter to maintain good health than in mild regions. Finally, the size of the hutch or other enclosure influences food consumption: a rabbit which can exercise daily in a roomy hutch usually shows a much healthier appetite than one kept in a small or crowded hutch.

In feeding your rabbits, you should consider these and other individual needs as they affect particular animals in the herd. An alert, conscientious breeder will not be content with giving, for instance, each one of his nursing does the same amount of feed, for even though they belong to the same variety and nurse litters of the same age and size, their individual requirements may still vary considerably. Too many beginners, it should be emphasized, tend to overfeed their rabbits, a pernicious practice resulting not only in much waste of feed, but also in making the animals sluggish and reluctant to breed. Overfed rabbits are usually poor producers.

Importance of Balanced Rations

The correct feed for rabbits is one balanced as to proteins, carbohydrates, fats, minerals, and vitamins. Its cost, if the rabbits are kept for profitable production, should be as low as possible. Since a wide variety of feeds, such as greens of many kinds, root crops, grains, leguminous hays, protein supplements, salt, dry bread and other table leftovers, furnish nutritious sustenance for rabbits, a well-balanced choice from these will provide sufficient proteins, carbohydrates, minerals, and vitamins.

Your rabbits must have protein-rich food regularly to build new body tissues or to repair worn-out tissues. Protein, as a primary tissue constituent, builds (so to say) bones, muscles, ligaments, hair, skin, and nails. A food ration lacking in protein will soon make itself felt in slow growth and reduced weight. Carbohydrates are energy and heat suppliers;

they come in the forms of sugars and starches. The woody fiber of carbohydrates with its bulk keeps the digestive tract in fit condition. Fat also supplies energy and heat, but in much greater amounts than carbohydrates. Minerals, more than a dozen of which the healthy animal body requires, help to produce and to repair certain tissues, especially teeth and bones. Vitamins, as is well known, serve as regulators of metabolism, the normal growth and condition of which they help to maintain. As such they are needful in the daily diet of all animal life. When selecting feeds for rabbits, their protein and carbohydrate contents are of most importance.

Fresh Greens a Natural Food for Rabbits

Among the most natural, nutritious, and inexpensive foods for rabbits are many kinds of greens, both cultivated and wild. Some authorities maintain that a mature rabbit can be maintained in good health on greens alone, since they are rich in proteins, minerals, and vitamins, especially vitamin A. Moreover, since their water content is very high, often ranging up to 90 percent, greens may be considered highly digestible. On some rabbit farms in Eastern Europe, where two thousand breeding does are kept under strict control, their principal feed for from seven to eight months of the year is grass. Only pregnant and nursing does are given, in addition, 30 to 40 grams of grains, mainly oats, and various kinds of hay.

If, perchance, you have access to greens in your backyard, garden, farm, or other accessible place, by all means utilize them to the best advantage, since they are not only palatable for your rabbits, but also lower the cost of feeding them.

The prominent role which fresh, clean greens play in a well-balanced feeding system is shown in a two-year experi-

ment conducted by the Swedish scientist S. Nordfeldt with
white landrabbits. One herd was given daily during the winter months the following mixture of dry feed: 65.9% hay
meal; 16.1% oatmeal; 16.2% wheat bran; 1.6% soybean meal;
0.2% minerals; and 0.2% cod-liver oil. This dry-feeding not
only lowered fertility, but caused cannibalism and other
losses. Among the surviving animals from 70% to 80% died.
The young suffered from general debility. The causes as-
signed were lack of vitamins and lack of water. When, in
another experiment, the 65.9% hay meal was replaced with
fresh-cut greens, including dandelion, timothy, and couch
grass, the other ingredients being retained, the rabbits re-
gained normal fertility and the young developed properly.
The thirteen does kept on dry feed had only six litters, three
of which were dead, with young totaling 39, eight of which
lived to be 28 days old. The second group of thirteen does,
fed also on greens, had eleven litters, all normal, with young
totaling 95, 91 of which lived to the 28th day.

When you feed greens to your rabbits, make sure that they
are absolutely fresh, clean, not mildewed, frosted, or in any
way spoiled. Those grown in the open, in sunny locations,
are best. They should not be kept in heaps, which will cause
heating, but loosely on a clean floor or in suitable racks. Wet
grass, provided that it is not moldy, is not harmful to rabbits.
Do not glut your rabbits with only one kind of greens, but
give them a variety in small quantities. If you change over
from dry to green feed, by all means do so gradually, giving
them, as part of their daily rations, only small amounts of
greens at first, so that their digestive systems may adjust
themselves readily to the change. Young, recently weaned
rabbits are especially sensitive to sudden changes in their
diet and should therefore be given greens at first only in very
small quantities.

Kinds of Greens

The varieties of greens suitable for domestic rabbits are almost unlimited, and they include both weeds and cultivated plants. Among common weeds are dandelions, which, mixed with other greens and fed in moderate amounts, are good for your rabbits. Cow parsnip, sometimes called hogweed, a very succulent plant, is particularly suitable for nursing does. Various wild clovers, with either white or pink blossoms, often found growing among short grasses, make valuable rabbit food. Watercress provides a tasty appetizer for rabbits that seem to need a safe, stimulating change in their diet. The common, yellow-blooming sow thistle, sometimes called milk thistle, may safely be fed to rabbits of all ages. Wild vetches are readily taken by rabbits. We should also mention mallow, chickweed, wild carrots, plantains, and, of course, fresh grasses. Among plants not to be fed to rabbits are oleander, goldenrod, castor bean, lupine, poppy, burdock, and others.

A very inexpensive rabbit food is furnished by kitchen leftovers, such as vegetable trimmings in the form of carrot and beet tops, lettuce leaves, potato peels, culled apples and other fruit, provided that none of these items is spoiled. Lawn clippings from grass not sprayed with insecticides are relished by rabbits.

Among cultivated greens good for rabbits may be mentioned Jerusalem artichokes, which are rich in sugar content and easily grown, sunflowers, Brussels sprouts, cauliflower, kohlrabi, cabbages, kales, parsley, and lettuce. Very desirable are leguminous plants, including alfalfa, lespedeza, clover, vetch, and others, and fed both as greens and as hays. Hays fed to rabbits should be green in color, leafy, fine-stemmed, well-cured, and, of course, neither dusty nor moldy. Both greens and hays are best placed in suitable racks, not on the floor of the hutch, where they soon get dirty and spoil. To facilitate feeding hays and other roughages and to avoid waste, they may be cut into three- or four-inch lengths.

During the winter months, various more or less juicy root crops, including carrots, beets, turnips, sugar beets, mangels, sweet potatoes, etc., furnish a welcome change in the rabbits' diet. Their need for gnawing may be met by giving them branches of fruit trees, also of acacias, poplars, willows, hazelnuts, and others.

Grain Feeding

Grains, such as oats, barley, buckwheat, milo, kaffir, rye, and the soft kinds of corn, may be fed either whole or milled. Their extensive use in feed rations depends on their quality, their ready availability, and, of course, on their cost. Oats and barley are usually rolled for mixing in mashes, thus avoiding waste. When they can be bought at low cost in suitable quantities, they should be stocked in good supply, because they are a good rabbit food. Flinty kinds of corn, that is, those with hard kernels, are best fed as meals. Some breeders assert that rabbits will eat whole oats readily, provided that they have first been "trained" by eating a mixture of whole corn, barley, and peas. These same authorities advocate feeding acorns for fattening rabbits—at first in small quantities, to get the rabbits used to them. By-products from the manufacture of grains, such as bran, shorts, and middlings, are usually included in meal mixtures and in pellets.

To balance rabbit rations, various protein-rich supplements, such as soybeans, peanuts, linseed, and others are available. They are fed as meals included in the usual rabbit pellets. Soybean, linseed, and cottonseed meals mixed in equal parts provide a satisfactory protein supplement.

Farmers' Bulletin 1730, titled "Rabbit Production," issued by the U.S. Department of Agriculture, details analyses of successfully used rabbit diets. For dry does, herd bucks, and developing young, the suggested rations should furnish:

Protein	12 to 15%
Fat	2 to 3.5%
Fiber	20 to 37%
Nitrogen-free extract	43 to 47%
Ash or mineral	5 to 6.5%

For pregnant and nursing does, the components of the ration should be:

Protein	16 to 20%
Fat	3 to 5.5%
Fiber	14 to 20%
Nitrogen-free extract	44 to 50%
Ash or mineral	4.5 to 6.5%

The protein content may run higher than above suggested without ill effect on the rabbits, provided only that the feed rations are otherwise well balanced.

To meet the rabbits' requirements for salt, spools or blocks of this mineral are conveniently fastened in the hutches and thus made always accessible. In their place, 0.5% to 1% of salt can be added to the pellets or the feed mixture.

Pellets Popular Rabbit Food

Owing to their convenience in handling, storing, and feeding, pellets for rabbits are available in many brands and in guaranteed formulas under such names as "all-purpose pellets," "tonic and conditioning pellets," and others. In the main, however, rabbit pellets fall into two classes: all-grain pellets, fed with hay, and the green or so-called complete pellets, the latter furnishing all nutriments for a balanced ration. Tags on sacks of manufactured pellets clearly indicate the guaranteed analyses. A commonly used manufactured pellet, to give an example, carries this analysis:

Crude protein, not below	16%
Crude fat, not below	3%
Crude fiber, not over	18%
Minerals, not over	12%

Once you have found a pellet or pellets which meet your cost requirements and the needs of your rabbits, then by all means continue their use.

At this point, I wish to comment briefly on a little-known eating habit of rabbits, often likened to cows chewing their cud, namely, their eating, usually early in the morning, most, if not all, of their soft manure. This is not the ordinary, usually hard manure produced during the day, but the soft manure produced during the night. It should be clearly understood that this pseudo-rumination is not a disease, but a normal habit and process.

Feeding Techniques

Whether you feed your rabbits once, twice, or thrice a day, regularity is most important. Rabbits come to know the time of feeding; not to feed them punctually means letting them go hungry longer than is good for them, which may affect their health. If you feed only once a day, then evening is the proper time, since by nature rabbits are night feeders. Twice-a-day feeding, mornings and evenings, is especially desirable when there are young to be fed. If feed is left uneaten from one meal to the next, then you should reduce the ration until you have determined the right quantity. At feeding time, be sure to note the condition of your rabbits and to adjust the quantity of feed accordingly. You can estimate a rabbit's physical condition by simply feeling how thinly or how thickly its ribs and backbone are covered with flesh; then, if need be, decrease or increase the amount of feed.

Feed rations should be suited to certain rabbits' particular needs. Thus to keep dry does, herd bucks not in service, and junior bucks and does in sound health, a not-so-rich ration is satisfactory. Often a good-quality legume hay that is leafy and fine-stemmed will be satisfactory.

According to Farmers' Bulletin No. 2121, of the U.S. Department of Agriculture, if grass or a coarse legume hay is fed, each eight-pound rabbit should have two ounces, or one-third cup of all-grain pellets or grain-protein mixture several times a week. Simple calculation will enable you to fix the right amounts of concentrates for other weights. Bucks in service should have the same amount of concentrates, and all the quality hay they want. Growing junior does and bucks may be full-fed on alfalfa pellets only, from the time of weaning to the time of breeding. Pregnant does may be given, in addition to choice hay, all the concentrates they will eat. A pelleted ration with no hay, or else all-grain pellets or a grain-protein mixture with hay, can be fed. When sudden changes are made in rations, some does will lose their appetites and go "off feed"; hence it is advisable to make such changes in a very gradual way. After kindling, the doe is kept on the same high-concentrate ration as before, except that the quantity is increased as her litter grows. When her young begin to eat, there should be some extra feed dishes in the hutch to prevent crowding. At this time, a small quantity of rolled oats and alfalfa hay is good for them. Greens should be given them very sparingly at first. Finally, if for reasons of time or labor-saving it should become needful to feed your entire herd but *one* ration, then the ration described above and suggested for does with nursing litters is likely to be quite satisfactory.

Hopper-Feeding and Hand-Feeding

Hopper- or self-feeding means keeping feed before the rabbits twenty-four hours a day. Experiments show that hopper-fed young rabbits at weaning time are heavier than hand-fed ones, and also that they require less feed to produce a given amount of live weight. Since feed to last for several days may be placed in the hopper, a saving in time and labor results. Besides, and this is important, there is neither waste nor contamination of feed. In general, hopper-feeding is practical when feeding complete pellets to pregnant does, does with nursing litters, and rabbits which are being readied for butchering.

Hand-feeding—putting the needed amount of feed each day in a crock or other suitable container—is usually practiced by hobbyists who keep but comparatively few rabbits and who enjoy "working with them." It is particularly suitable for those rabbits whose rations must be limited, such as herd bucks, dry does, and overweight animals.

Creep-Feeding for Early Weaning

The so-called creep ration, fairly recently developed, is special feed in easily digested form to enable young rabbits to make a satisfactory initial transition from doe's milk to feed. It is available under various trade names at feed-supply stores. Fed to youngsters from the 21st day on, it is meant to reduce mortality, quite frequent at this age, increase weaning weights, and relieve nursing does which under severe weather stress tend to give less milk. The more milk a doe produces, the less creep feed is eaten by the young. Likewise, as the youngsters grow and adjust to the regular adult feed, they eat less and less of the high-energy creep ration. The use of creep rations tends also to place much less production stress on the does, enabling them to maintain their physical vigor more readily.

CHAPTER SEVEN

Selling Surplus Rabbits

Rabbit Meat as a Commercial Product
Selling Live Rabbits
White Rabbits Preferred
Selling to Commercial Buyers
Selling Show Stock

S ELLING or marketing surplus rabbits usually implies offer-
ing them for sale in considerable quantities at more or
less regular intervals. Meant primarily for hobbyists, whose
prime purpose in keeping rabbits is pleasure rather than
profit, this book makes no pretense of giving detailed information on massbreeding, slaughtering, and selling rabbits for
meat and fur as a commercial venture. These are strictly
business operations conducted to make money for the entre-
preneur, who will discontinue them promptly when they fail
to show substantial financial gains at the end of the year.
Furthermore, the establishment and the operation of even
a fair-sized commercial rabbit farm require a considerable
financial investment, including usually the employment of
extra help, neither of which requirements appeals to the average hobbyist. In most cases, he is content with maintaining
a small, select herd of high-quality animals, care of which he
and members of his immediate family can accomplish to their
enjoyment during leisure hours.

Rabbit Meat as a Commercial Product

Today rabbit meat as a commercial product is certainly not produced in the large quantities of yesteryear, when it was a favorite item on the daily menus of good restaurants and hotels in many parts of the country. Of course, in those early days the mass production in batteries of chicken meat was still in its infancy. In other words, rabbit meat served in public eating places did not have to face the very sharp competition which today chicken meat provides in growing measure. And as long as chicken meat can be produced more efficiently and more cheaply than rabbit meat, the latter will necessarily have to take a back seat wherever in markets, restaurants, hotels, etc., various kinds of meats are offered to the public.

Domestic rabbit meat, it should be emphasized, is very digestible, carrying a high percentage of proteins, and in food value is comparable to beef. The quality of a particular rabbit's meat depends on the age of the animal, the kind and grade of feed it got, and in general, on the over-all care it received during its life. This meat has a distinctive flavor which connoisseurs of good food rate well above that of chicken and many other meats. Owing to its palatability, rabbit meat is frequently included in the special diets given ailing persons at convalescent homes and hospitals. To the hobbyist and the backyard livestock-keeper, rabbit meat brings a delicious, welcome change to the daily menu, for which otherwise he might have to pay a big price, especially in parts of the country where but few domestic rabbits are being raised. This meat carries a delicate flavor, is white, small-boned, and seldom very fat.

In this connection it is interesting to note that the consumption of domestic rabbit meat in France, England, Germany, and other European countries is very much higher than in this country, due largely to the fact that in those countries there are literally thousands of small households depending on rabbit culture to provide meat for the family table. Moreover, the practice of directly and indirectly breeding domestic rabbits for exhibition purposes in these same countries has resulted in national and international shows boasting thousands of entries, thus testifying pointedly to the popularity of the domestic rabbit as a national hobby. Since rabbits in European countries are being kept today under much more sanitary conditions than was the case ten or twenty years ago, and since this pertinent fact has been repeatedly impressed on the general public through the press and other communication channels, the sale of rabbit meat has shown a steady and surprising increase.

Selling Live Rabbits

Selling surplus rabbits is often not as simple as it appears on the surface. For the hobbyist and keeper of small herds, selling them alive is undoubtedly the easiest and least bothersome way of realizing at least a fair financial return. If but few surplus animals are to be sold, friends of the family and neighbors may oftentimes be induced to take them more or less regularly. Scientific laboratories and biology departments in schools, if not too distant, offer a good and steady outlet for live rabbits. In most cases, they are quite particular as to the kind, age, weight, and number of rabbits they require at stated times. Any rabbit breeder catering to this rather well-paying market should obtain detailed and exact information on the buyer's requirements, which, if possible, he should then meet specifically and promptly. If, for example, a certain laboratory is in the market for 10, 100, or more animals of a certain breed, age, weight, color, and sex monthly, the seller will have to supply the exact number and quality, even if he has to pick up some from other rabbitries, else lose this market. Moreover, laboratories will accept only truly healthy animals, often reserving the right to inspect the seller's installation and premises to make sure that his animals are kept in clean, sanitary hutches and that the herd is healthy and of uniform quality. Some laboratories go so far as to prescribe the type and quality of self-cleaning cages in which rabbits meant for them should be kept.

White Rabbits Preferred

More or less apropos here may be the advice of an old-timer writing in a recent issue of a rabbit magazine, "If the hobbyist wants to make a little money with his rabbits, he should by all means select a white breed, such as the New Zealand Whites or the Californians. And the reason: the white pelts are worth much more than any colored pelts. Also white fryers generally sell for from two to three cents more per pound live weight, which means a substantial amount if you do not do your own butchering. Fur manufacturers can take a white pelt and dye it the most beautiful tints, as for making ladies' jackets, slippers, and the like, for boudoir use. By shearing, dyeing, and tinting a white rabbit pelt, they can imitate at least nine different kinds of high-priced furs, including Silver, Black, and Blue Fox, Sables, and Martens. While a colored rabbit pelt is simply a colored pelt with limited uses, a white pelt has almost unlimited uses. So it really pays to raise white rabbits."

Selling to Commercial Buyers

In certain regions of this country, the large commercial rabbitries, slaughterhouses, and rabbit growers' associations maintain long-established markets for which they buy up live rabbits from small and other breeders, if they meet certain requirements as to weight and color. They dispatch their trucks regularly for this purpose on established routes. Some cooperative rabbit associations operate slaughterhouses to which members as well as non-members can deliver their surplus stock for cash. Some years ago this writer disposed of surplus stock regularly to such a buyer, as did some of his fellow rabbit-keepers. Perhaps the main drawback of selling live rabbits for meat and fur to various wholesale buyers lies in the price-control which these business firms are able to exercise in the market. In other words, they usually offer a set price per pound of live weight for rabbits of certain sizes, ages, and colors. The seller either takes or leaves this set price, since he is in no position to bargain, no matter how fine the quality of his rabbits happens to be. The profit which he realizes under such and similar conditions is usually modest; however, he is relieved of feeding surplus animals at a loss, and of all further effort to sell them. It is generally true also that the average rabbit-keeper lacks the required salesmanship so-called, as well as the initiative to market his stock profitably, for he is mainly a grower and producer, not a merchandiser and seller, the points of view and aims of these two groups being entirely different.

Selling Show Stock

Some hobbyists specialize in one or two breeds of fancy domestic rabbits with a view to producing one or more exhibition strains. This is at once a fascinating enterprise calling for a thorough and practical knowledge of breed characteristics, behavior, and exhibition possibilities. It takes quite a number of years of patient, intelligent effort to achieve a quality strain of fancy rabbits. The breed or breeds kept should preferably be popular ones, insuring spirited competition at local, district, and national shows. Repeated wins of top prizes gained under such conditions, with ensuing favorable publicity in the local press and especially in rabbit and small-stock magazines are bound to lend the exhibitor's name growing prestige among members of breeders' clubs and rabbit enthusiasts in general. Such recognition, however, is usually not sufficient to bring enough sales of breeding stock to render the enterprise profitable. What is needed is publicity of the right sort at the right time—more or less continuous advertising in the logical media, including, of course, rabbit and small-stock magazines. If, as a result, a good many sales can be effected locally, well and good, since the buyers can select their purchases personally and take them with them. In many instances, however, the advertising is bound to attract sales-inquiries from buyers living at such distances from the advertiser as to make shipping necessary. This, of course, necessitates the making of special shipping crates for the rabbits, which over long distances are usually sent by air-express collect to shorten their time en route. Since rabbits are very sensitive to heat, they are best dispatched during cool weather, the customer being notified promptly in advance of the exact shipping date and the method of shipping, that is, railway express or air-express, the latter method being considerably more expensive.

While it takes a number of years for a breeder specializing in the sale of high-grade breeding stock to build up a steady business in the manner suggested above, if he succeeds in doing so, it should yield him a good profit, since prices charged for high-quality breeding stock of well-advertised strains are usually quite high. Moreover, the longer he stays in business, the more goodwill his activities are likely to generate, with satisfied customers telling interested friends and fellow breeders of their favorable purchases, thus directly or indirectly recommending the stock of the specialist breeder. Proof that such part-time or full-time businesses are in continuous and presumably profitable operation is found in the advertising columns of rabbit and small-stock periodicals, where these expert rabbit breeders offer their stock for sale.

CHAPTER EIGHT

Practical Suggestions on Various Topics

Shows and Their Value

If it were not for local, district, and national shows, the rabbit hobby would be without its most potent stimulus. Over the years, rabbit shows have been instrumental in the organization of specialty clubs, since on these pleasant occasions, breeders specializing in this or that variety come together to exhibit their finest specimens and in general to promote their favorite breed. Rabbit shows have been instrumental also, directly and indirectly, in the practical application of breed standards of perfection by competent judges, as well as in the continuing improvement of these standards. Moreover, new breeds of domestic rabbits usually make their first public appearance in the show-room, where they may or may not win real and permanent following.

For the novice just starting with rabbits, the show parades

before his eyes a wide variety of fascinating, high-quality animals—all in one accessible, convenient location, where he can admire and compare them to his heart's content and with no one to bother or to prejudice him, as might well be the case at some private rabbitry. Here at the show he can observe also the judging of the different breeds, ask questions concerning their relative merits, and in general inform himself on the current trends in modern rabbit culture. Finally, as a practical follow-up to his visit at the shows, he can call on individual exhibitors whose names and addresses he gleaned from the identity cards fastened to the show cages.

For the old-timer, the show, in addition to keeping him abreast of the quality of his favorite breed or breeds as exhibited, is an informal social event of the first order. For there old friendships are eagerly renewed and new friendships made on the basis of sincere, common interests. More rabbit fanciers are "born" at shows than anywhere else, for there the newcomer, showing a liking for this or that breed, can get sound advice on its merits from the expert, the old-timer, the exhibitor, or even from the judge.

At the larger shows, specialty clubs usually hold their annual meetings, which give members and visitors every opportunity to exchange views on every fundamental aspect of rabbit-keeping in a thoroughly congenial atmosphere and to find in friendly discussions solutions to problems sought for some time. At shows where meat rabbits are placed on display in considerable numbers, demonstrations are often given of slaughtering, of evaluating the meat of the carcass, and of displaying rabbit meat in various appetizing dishes. To acquaint the public with tasty rabbit meat, samples may be offered. At other shows, fur classes may be the featured attraction, with special exhibits of rabbit wool in its different grades, and of coats, jackets, and the like made of rabbit furs.

Readying Rabbits for Shows

Rabbits intended for exhibition should be selected well in advance of the actual show date, so that they may be suitably conditioned. Only specimens typical of their particular breed and in top physical condition should be considered for showing. Their feeding should be so managed that they will be in perfect physical condition at show time. If their appetites need tempting, some fresh greens, dry bread, or bread and milk may be given. Most exhibitors groom their show rabbits by hand, moving from head to tail to rid the coat of dead hairs and dust, and to give the coat some luster. Rabbits in heavy molt should not be considered for show purposes. To ensure the rabbits being tame and tractable on the judging table, they should be handled frequently long before show time. If white varieties are to be exhibited, they should be kept in spick-and-span hutches. Hutch and other stains on white rabbits may be removed by applying some bleach, as peroxide. French chalk or talcum is also useful for this purpose. The novice exhibitor should learn how to pose his particular breed from an experienced exhibitor. Teaching a rabbit to pose readily on the judging table greatly facilitates the judge's work. Belgian Hare breeders especially find it needful to train their animals to pose at the show, so that at a snap of the fingers or a short, sharp whistle, they will freeze into the right position.

Shipping Rabbits

Over reasonably short distances, rabbits may be shipped by railway express. Over long distances, air-express is preferable since it shortens the time in transit very appreciably. Air-express costs much more than railway express. If you are sure that the rabbits will go through to their final destination on *one* plane, then by all means ship by air. Since rabbits are greatly discomforted by heat, they are best not shipped during hot weather. If the shipment has to be routed over two airlines, the air-freight may be double. It is advisable therefore to inquire beforehand at the express office what the shipping cost, which the buyer customarily pays on receipt of the shipment, will be.

Durable but lightweight boxes or crates are suitable for shipping rabbits. A few handfuls of straw are placed in the crate for bedding. A small water-can is wired on the inside of the shipping crate, and a small hole is cut through the top of the crate directly over the location of the can, marked "Water here!" Or some cabbage, carrots, or potatoes may be placed in the crate. A can with pellets is fastened into a corner, and a feedbag tied to the top of the shipping crate with instructions for feeding en route. A piece of fairly large cardboard tacked to the top of the box or crate and marked in large, red letters, "Live Rabbits! Do not delay!" helps to call the express clerks' attention to the urgency of the shipment. The shipper should notify the buyer, well in advance of the actual shipment, of the date he will ship the rabbits, giving, if desirable, also the number of the flight, in the case of air-express, the name of the airline, and the probable time of arrival at destination. This information is meant to enable the buyer to be at home when the rabbits arrive or to make suitable preparations for their arrival at destination.

Membership in Rabbit Clubs

Any rabbit fancier, but especially the beginner, will find membership in a specialty or general club highly stimulating and beneficial. First of all, he would do well to join the American Rabbit Breeders' Association, whose secretary maintains headquarters at 4323 Murray Avenue in Pittsburgh, Pa., 15219. In return for the nominal membership fee he will receive the monthly ARBA Bulletin, which will keep him well informed on conventions, shows, registrations, specialty clubs, and numerous other worthwhile activities. The bulletin is written in an informal, personal style making for leisurely reading.

From the secretary of the ARBA, any fancier can obtain a list of specialty breed clubs and associations, whose secretaries are prepared to send pertinent information regarding their organizations to prospective members. Moreover, most specialty clubs issue newsletters more or less regularly to their members, featuring news items and articles detailing the advantages of breeding New Zealands, Californians, or whatever variety happens to be sponsored by the club. Furthermore, there are generally many personal items from individual members telling of their successes with rabbits, with housing and certain equipment, detailing unusual experiences, and asking pertinent questions. This writer has examined quite a number of club bulletins and newsletters and finds them both informative and interesting.

Membership in a specialty club gives the novice fancier a feeling of belonging to a group of men and women maintaining and furthering a pleasant, common interest. Preferably such a club should be well represented in his locality, or not far from there, so that he may attend its meetings regularly and so become personally acquainted with fellow breeders. Problems concerning feeding, breeding, and other essential phases of rabbit culture are bound to come up in the beginner's experience—problems for the solutions of which he should be able to turn to experienced local fanciers. What better way than to meet and to talk with these men at club meetings, where usually an atmosphere of cooperation and enthusiasm reigns, and where long-experienced members are glad to welcome and to help the novice fancier make a satisfactory start with his rabbits? Many clubs stage table shows at their meetings designed to aid members in applying the many provisions of breed standards to living examples. Various demonstrations, as of labor-saving devices, even of slaughtering, etc., may be featured on the monthly club program. *Last,* but by no means *least,* most clubs engage in social activities quite regularly, with local shows and picnics in the summertime, and dinners and dances at other times, as well as with visits to members' rabbitries. All these informal and friendly club affairs will certainly aid the novice fancier in mastering the finer points of breeding his favorite kind of rabbits, given in an atmosphere of helpfulness and cordial competition.

Cooperative Rabbit Organizations

Cooperatives, so-called, formed by groups of breeders of livestock have not been successful in many instances owing largely to a lack of businesslike leadership and willingness on the part of individual members to shoulder important responsibilities. There are, of course, notable exceptions to this general rule, such as the following case, which appeared in *The National Rabbit Raiser* magazine, and which is here presented in somewhat abbreviated form:

In 1962, the Lakehead Cooperative Rabbit Industries were organized in Esko, Minnesota, with an initial membership of forty, approximately half of whom are active today. Lyle Colberg functions as manager of the group.

This cooperative buys from its members strictly on the basis of grade. Currently the purchase price of grade No. 1 rabbit is 25¢ per pound, live weight. The grade or quality is determined by the size of the loin, the amount of fat, and the age of the rabbit. To be graded No. 1, the weight of the rabbit must be from four to five pounds, and its age not exceeding ten weeks. The size of the loin and the fat content can be judged by feeling the rabbit carefully, while age within a week can be determined by the condition of the teeth, toenails, body, etc.

Paid employes as such this cooperative does not keep. All work involving butchering, packaging, and marketing is done by the members during off-hours from their regular jobs. Usually they work in teams of two or three, the processing being done at the Esko cooperative locker plant, but with the Lakehead Cooperative Rabbit Industries' own equipment. The rabbit meat is packed in sealed plastic bags, which in turn are placed in attractive and colorful boxes for meat-case display in stores. As far as by-products are concerned, the skins are dried and sold for ten cents each; the fertilizer is sold to flower gardeners at $2.25 the sackfull. Each doe kept by the membership is expected to yield a clear monthly profit of one dollar.

In 1963 this cooperative processed 2500 rabbits valued at $3000. Thus far, all earnings have been plowed back into the business to pay for various equipment, including wash tanks, chill tanks, chill baskets, butcher knives, locker carts, scales, sealing irons, and numerous other items. The end of 1964 showed a small surplus; at that time all equipment was paid for. The cooperative makes a series of "Tested Rabbit Recipes" available to the consumer.

Development Contests Stimulate Interest

Development contests are annual affairs staged by several rabbit clubs in Colorado. One of their principal purposes is the measurement of the growth and development of young rabbits between the ages of two months and five months. Each rabbit is judged three times before final placings are made. All breeds may compete in this contest and are judged by their particular breed standard. Special emphasis is placed on the gain in weight and the development of the body from one judging to the next, with the weights being compared for the three judgings.

There are awards for the best individual rabbit and for best display, which may include as many as three rabbits. At each judging, each rabbit is awarded a certain number of points for that particular month. The points are added to determine the winners at the completion of the third and final judging. The animal receiving the most points is the winner. In the best-display class, points are awarded on the basis of the exhibitor. Each person may enter as many as three rabbits. The exhibitor whose total entry receives the most points is the winner. The development contest has greatly helped to keep interest in the Colorado rabbit clubs alive.

Tested Recipes for Cooking Domestic Rabbit Meat

(Courtesy of American Rabbit Breeders' Association, Inc.)

To prepare the meat for cooking, keep it in the refrigerator for a few hours, or else in cold water. Then wash it in cold water, patting it dry with a clean towel. Cut the rabbit in eight or ten pieces (if it is not to be cooked whole) by first disjointing the legs, cutting the hind legs in two pieces, if desired, and the body in four pieces. When preparing "Ready to Cook" fryers, follow the directions given on the package.

Fried Rabbit—Use fryer size only. Make a batter, using the following ingredients for each rabbit: 1 egg, ½ cup of flour, ½ cup of milk, and ¼ teaspoon salt. Beat eggs, add the milk and the salt, and stir into the flour to make a smooth batter. Wipe the rabbit with a clean, damp cloth and cut into pieces of the right size for serving. Dip each piece into the batter, making sure that it is thoroughly coated. In an iron skillet, heat well-flavored fat until it is hot enough to set the batter quickly. Just brown the pieces of rabbit evenly, then reduce the heat, and cook at a lower temperature for 20 to 30 minutes, or until tender. Serve on a hot platter and garnish with parsley.

Roast Rabbit—Use any large rabbit, aged three months or older. Make a dressing the same as you would for chicken or turkey; stuff; place in covered baking dish or pan. Add 1 cup of water in pan and steam-roast, placing 4 or 5 strips of salt pork or bacon over the rabbit. Baste often. Roast slowly for 2½ hours. Turn rabbit three or four times. If it is very large, then roast it for three hours slowly.

Savory Rabbit—Wash the rabbit and cut into pieces. Dredge with 4 tablespoons of flour, 2 teaspoons of salt, and ⅛ teaspoon of pepper. Brown in 4 tablespoons of bacon or other fat. Remove meat; place it in stewpan and cover with boiling water; add 1 medium-size onion cut into small pieces and 2 bay leaves. Cook slowly until nearly tender. To the fat that was used to brown the rabbit, add 2 tablespoons of flour, mix thoroughly, and add 1 cup of vinegar. Pour this sauce over the meat and simmer until it is very tender. Serve with dumplings. This makes an excellent meal served with fresh or canned string beans and with a dessert of baked apples.

Braised Rabbit—Use 1 rabbit, whole; 1 cup cooked rice; 1 tablespoon olive oil; 2 eggs; 1 cup (plus) brown gravy; ¼ lb. chopped mushrooms; 1 chopped onion; ¼ lb. sausage meat; 1 glass of wine, pepper and salt. Combine all ingredients, except gravy and wine, and stuff the rabbit with them.

Sew it up, flour it well, put it in a casserole with the gravy and wine (any cooking wine will do). Cover and simmer for 2 hours. A garnish of fried sausages is good with this recipe.

Smothered Rabbit—Wipe rabbit with clean, damp cloth. Cut it into pieces. Cover with hot water, then simmer for about one hour in partly covered kettle. Transfer the pieces of meat to a shallow baking dish; cover with a sauce made of one cup of the liquid, one cup of milk thickened with four tablespoons of butter blended with two tablespoons of flour. Season with salt and pepper. Bake in moderate oven, about 350° F. for one-half hour, or until meat is tender, and serve in a baking dish. Young rabbit may be put directly into the baking dish, covered with two cups of the thin sauce made with milk, and baked until tender.

Rabbit Stew with Vegetables—Use 1 rabbit, weighing about 3 lbs., 4 medium-sized potatoes cut into quarters, 4 large carrots cubed, 1 medium-sized onion, 3 tablespoons of flour, 3 teaspoons of salt, and a few grains of pepper. Wash the rabbit carefully, cut in into pieces, cover with cold water, and allow to boil slowly until almost tender. Add the potatoes, carrots, onions, or other vegetables, and cook until tender. Add the seasoning and flour moistened in a little cold water. Stir until the liquid surrounding the stew is slightly thickened and serve at once.

Rabbit Salad—3 cups of diced cooked rabbit meat; 3 cups of diced celery, 2 tablespoons capers, 1 teaspoon onion juice, 1 cup thick mayonnaise, paprika, ½ cup of salad oil, ¼ cup of vinegar, salt, and a dash of tabasco sauce. To the diced meat, add the oil, vinegar, onion juice, salt as needed, and paprika.

Let stand in a cold place for three or four hours, or overnight. Then add the celery, capers, tabasco sauce, and enough mayonnaise to cover well. Serve on crisp lettuce or other salad greens with a garnish of olives and radishes.

Rabbit à la King—1 rabbit or 3 cups of diced cooked meat, 2 cups of cream, 4 tablespoons butter, 2 tablespoons of flour, 1 teaspoon of minced onion, 1 lb. chopped mushrooms, 1 tablespoon of lemon juice, ½ cup of chopped pimentos. Wipe the dressed rabbit with a clean, damp cloth. Place it on a rack in a saucepan. Add ½ teaspoon salt, barely cover with hot water, partly cover saucepan, then simmer 1½ to 2 hours, or until done. Let cool in the liquid, drain, remove meat from bones, then cut into even pieces. Heat the cream in a double boiler. Blend the flour with 2 tablespoons butter, stir into the cream until thick. Melt the remaining butter in a skillet; add the green pepper and the mushrooms. Cook a few minutes over low heat. Beat the egg yolks, then stir a small part of the thick cream into them and add the remainder of the sauce. Now add the mushrooms, green pepper, onion, and lemon juice, with paprika and salt and pepper to taste. Add the diced meat and pimento. When thoroughly heated, serve the mixture in patty shells or on crisp toast.

Rabbit, German Style—Singe the rabbit after it has been carefully cleaned, and wash it through several changes of cold water. Cut it into five pieces, that is, remove the saddle, make two pieces of the hindquarters, and two of the forequarters. Fry ¼ lb. of bacon until the fat is well fried out. Put the rabbit in; turn it until it is brown; then dust it with salt and pepper. Cover it with another pan and bake it in a quick oven for about 1 hour. Dish the rabbit; add to the pan two tablespoons of butter, stirring the butter until brown; then add two tablespoons of potato flour, mix well, and add a pint of sour cream; stir until boiling; add a teaspoon of salt and a dash of pepper, and pour it over the rabbit.

Mrs. Melvin W. Birkren, who, with her husband, operates the M & H Rabbitry at Fort Myers, Florida, recommends these tested recipes:

Rabbit Sausage—Grind together one-half rabbit meat and one-half pork (fat), add sage, poultry seasoning OR garlic. Also salt and pepper.

Sandwich Spread—Using old rabbit, boil until meat falls off the bones; add onions, olives, dill pickles, sweet pickles; grind all together and add mayonnaise to taste.

Roast Rabbit—Place rabbit in flat pan and cover with tomato or mushroom soup and roast.

CHAPTER NINE

Disease Control

Suggestions for Keeping Rabbits Healthy

Anyone who, like this writer, has kept domestic rabbits for a considerable period of time, is convinced that given reasonably good and regular care, these gentle animals will rarely cause their owner trouble through sickness. In other words, the problem of disease in domestic rabbits is best solved by anticipating and forestalling it through taking commonsense precautions long before it may threaten. The most common conditions contributing to rabbits getting sick are overcrowding, dirty hutches, dirty feeders and drinkers, and faulty management in general, in particular wrong feeding. Their owner should prevent these conditions from endangering the health of his herd *when he first starts keeping it;* for once they have caused serious trouble and disease, prevention is usually too late.

In their enthusiasm and eagerness to make a big, showy start, many hobbyists, especially young people, soon find themselves with far too many rabbits on hand for the available hutch or other accommodations. Crowded into wholly inadequate space, the animals lack fresh air and also sufficient room in which to exercise and to develop normally. And unless self-cleaning cages are used, the heavy accumulation of droppings and urine will soon wet the smelly bedding with consequent bad effects on the occupants. Where many rabbits, especially youngsters, are packed close together day and night for weeks at a time, there disease, once it gets a foothold, will spread fast, and usually with fatal results. For this reason every precaution should be taken to provide ample living and exercise space in sanitary surroundings for each and every rabbit kept.

Assuming that the novice has started out with good, healthy stock, he should then make every intelligent and persistent effort to see to it that it *stays healthy and vigorous.* He should remember that domestic rabbits, or for that matter any other domestic animals, in normal health are much less susceptible to disease than animals lacking good health; and if they do get sick, they are more likely to recover fully. Good health in rabbits is evidenced by clear eyes, a coat that is glossy and lustrous with natural bloom, an excellent appetite, and, finally, lively behavior. Such rabbits do not huddle together listlessly in a corner of the hutch: they are alert and active and take an interest in their immediate surroundings.

Domestic rabbits can be greatly aided in keeping healthy and strong by giving them the right food and drink in sanitary containers, and by housing them in self-cleaning hutches or cages. In other words, careful, humane management of the animals day in and day out is effective prevention of disease. The feeders and the drinkers should be washed regularly in hot, soapy water, then rinsed well in fresh water and left to dry, if possible, in the sun. Various utensils, such as scrapers, brushes, brooms, and others, should be put to soak in a pail with disinfectant for several hours. Following their use, nestboxes should be well disinfected, the bedding being either buried or burned so that it will not attract flies. Rabbit droppings should also be promptly disposed of. The smell emanating from them under the hutches can be eliminated by a sprinkling of fresh quicklime.

The alert fancier who knows his rabbits well will promptly catch sight of any that appear sluggish, inactive, or otherwise not up to their usually lively, normal behavior. As soon as he discovers them, he should by all means quarantine them in separate, clean cages located at some distance from all the other cages, until such a time as he is fully convinced that they no longer show symptoms of sickness and therefore present no danger of infection to his herd. Meanwhile he should make every attempt to locate the source of any infection or other trouble. Rabbits recently purchased or sent back from exhibitions, does returned from mating at other rabbitries, as well as faulty feeding, poor ventilation, and sudden changes in temperature—any of these may be responsible for a rabbit's listless or otherwise abnormal behavior.

Whether to treat an ailing rabbit or to destroy it depends on many factors. To be at all effective, treatment presupposes a sound knowledge of rabbit ailments, their probable seriousness, and their danger to the herd as a whole, and, of course, the correct use of available remedies. Unless an ailing rabbit is valuable, as in the case of an outstanding, proven show winner, it may not be worth the trouble and time to attempt a cure, for a rabbit recovered from a serious sickness rarely regains its former vigor and attractive appearance. If a cure

is attempted, then every effort should be made to nurse the
ailing animal, which frequently evidences loss of appetite,
back to health by tempting it with some succulent fresh
greens or other high-quality food. Medications are usually
given with the food, or else with some water.

In a book of this nature, meant mainly for beginners and
hobbyists in general, it is hardly advisable to list in detail
the numerous rabbit diseases, their symptoms, and their possible cures; hence some general comments on a few of the
more common ailments are given below. Certainly the rabbit
fancier should not attempt to be his own veterinarian. Post
mortem examinations made in scientific laboratories at reasonable rates are today readily available to fanciers almost
everywhere. The suggestions usually accompanying such
post mortems should prove most helpful in aiding rabbit-
keepers to improve the conditions pertaining to the health
of their herds. For many known rabbit ailments, effective
treatments are not as yet available. For this reason it is less
risky to destroy a number of sick rabbits than to attempt to
treat and cure them, and this applies particularly to those
suffering from respiratory infections.

Some More or Less Common Rabbit Ailments

Sore Hocks tend to afflict rabbits belonging to the "nervous"
breeds. A rough or a wet floor, or damp bedding, may cause
inflamed, even ulcerated pads of the hind feet. A rabbit so
troubled will often shake its feet and lick them. If no cure is
effected, the animal soon loses weight and vitality. Mild cases
of sore hocks are relieved simply by keeping the pads of the
feet dry, which means changing the bedding often. Letting
the rabbit run on clean, dry soil is another proven remedy.
In the more serious cases, the affected pads are thoroughly
cleaned with warm water and soap, then dried, and finally

daubed with iodine ointment once a day or so until the inflammation is gone. Sore hocks are not an inherited, but an acquired, ailment.

Colds are caused by various infections, which may prompt the animal to sneeze and to rub its nose with the front feet and the legs. There may be a clear, thin discharge from the nose, which when spread on the front legs soils and disarranges the fur. Isolation, strict sanitation, and proper feeding may relieve this condition, which can, because of its contagiousness, cause many rabbits to die.

Ear Mange is caused by a very small mite living on the inside of the external ear and causing both irritation and tissue wounds. The infection releases a fluid that hardens into scabs or crusts, below which the mites thrive. This disorder is evidenced by these symptoms: the affected animal tries to scratch its ears with its hind feet, and it shakes its head often; the ears are sore and filled with scabs. To clear this condition up, a soothing ear lotion consisting of one part iodoform, ten parts of ether, and twenty-five parts of olive oil, should be applied to the inflamed area, then repeated a week or so later until the scabs have completely healed. For prevention, hutches, nestboxes, and all utensils should be thoroughly disinfected.

Mucoid Enteritis is a mucus-like inflammation of the intestinal tract, also called bloat, which affects especially young rabbits. It is not contagious. The affected animal loses appetite, refuses food, grinds its teeth, sits in a huddled position, and drinks much water. It may be troubled with constipation or with diarrhea. In the latter case, there will be a discharge of a clear, jelly-like mucus. Treatment consists of feeding does nursing litters a ration containing an antibiotic supplement from the time the babies leave the nest until they are of weaning age. Such a ration is usually obtainable at the rabbit-feed supply store. For this disease there is as yet no recognized control.

Vent Disease, also called spirochetosis, refers simply to sores on the vent and sexual parts, which at times grow into a large mass. Infection occurs when a healthy rabbit is mated to a diseased one. Control of this ailment consists of rubbing the sore areas daily, for a week or so, with a calomel-lanoline ointment (one part of calomel to three parts of lanoline), obtainable at drugstores. Rabbits so treated should not be mated until the lesions have healed entirely. Prevention consists simply of examining bucks and does prior to mating.

Similar in appearance to the vent disease is so-called "urine burn" or "hutch burn," an inflammation of the vent region caused by the rabbits sitting on urine-soaked hutch floors. A clean hutch with dry bedding or one equipped with a self-cleaning floor will prevent this nuisance. Cases of "hutch burn" are best handled by cleaning the affected parts with an antiseptic solution, then applying an antiseptic ointment.

Myxomatosis is an extremely infectious, usually fatal virus disease spread mainly by biting insects, such as mosquitoes and ticks. Among the symptoms are swelling about the head, especially the eyes, ears, and nose, accompanied by a discharge of pus. The affected animal rapidly grows listless and inactive, and it has difficulty breathing. There is no practical remedy for this disease. For preventive purposes, all sick animals should be killed, then burned or buried. Nestboxes, bedding, and leftover feed should also be burned. Any animals exposed should be quarantined for several weeks and at a distance from the rabbitry, which should be screened against mosquitoes.

Coccidiosis usually causes heavy losses among young rabbits by attacking the liver or the intestines. The animals become infested with a microscopic parasite by taking contaminated food or water, or by licking their dirty feet, fur, or even hutch utensils. Among the symptoms is loss of weight, often accompanied by diarrhea. The coat loses its luster and becomes rather stiff. The rabbit sits in a huddled position. In the incipient stage of coccidiosis, the use of 1% of sulphamethazine in a mash may be effective, especially for the intestinal infection. Preventive measures include the use of self-cleaning floors, sanitary feeders and drinkers, and avoidance of overcrowding.

Pneumonia, or inflammation of the lungs, may afflict rabbits kept in damp, drafty, poorly ventilated, or overcrowded quarters, or subjected to sudden changes in temperatures. Animals so affected sit about quietly and show no appetite. Their breathing is slow and labored, their pulse fast and weak. When treated in its early stages, pneumonia can be relieved by injections of certain penicillin medications. Advanced cases usually prove fatal within a week.

As emphasized already, the best prevention against rabbit diseases is good management, which includes the use of quality feed, clean hutches and accessories, and regular care. All these essentials contribute to raising and keeping well-nourished, healthy animals, whose strong, firm bodies tend to resist most of the ordinary ailments.

Index